A TALE OF TWO
ECONOMIES

BY THE SAME AUTHOR

Safe as Houses? A Historical Analysis of Property Prices (London Publishing Partnership 2011)

Architect of Prosperity: Sir John Cowperthwaite and the making of Hong Kong (London Publishing Partnership 2017)

A TALE OF TWO ECONOMIES

Hong Kong, Cuba and the Two Men Who Shaped Them

NEIL MONNERY

GULIELMUS OCCAMUS & CO. LTD

Published by Gulielmus Occamus & Co. Ltd

ISBN: 978-1-913377-00-7

A catalogue record for this book is available from the British Library

Cover design by James Shannon

First edition (November 2019)

CONTENTS

INTRODUCTION

As the world entered the turbulent 1960s, two men, half a world apart, one a doctor and the other a classicist, both foreigners far from home, were charged with shaping the economic strategy of their adopted countries. More than half a century later, their principles still drive the economic policies of those countries to-day. They held a common objective. Both were determined to create a better world. And both were deeply thoughtful about how to discharge that heavy responsibility. But their proposed solutions could not have been more different.

One, Che Guevara, is well known as a revolutionary, active in Latin America and Africa before he was killed in Bolivia in 1967. He was central to Fidel Castro coming to power in Cuba and is an icon of revolutionary politics. He is less well known as the key architect of Cuba's economic system. And yet he spent many years establishing Cuban economic policy in roles such as Minister of Industry, President of the National Bank of Cuba, member of the three-member National Directorate of ORI (directing economic development), member of the Council of Ministers and lead negotiator for Cuba with the communist bloc. Even though Che the guerrilla fighter is better known than Che the civil servant, he was as serious about economics and its effect on society as he was about revolutionary warfare. Drawing on Marx,

Lenin, Mao and others, he developed a distinctly Cuban economic approach blending socialism and communism, emphasizing the role of the individual in crafting a new world.

The other, John Cowperthwaite, is largely unknown today. And yet he was fundamental to Hong Kong's economic recovery after World War II (Monnery 2017). He ran the Department for Supplies, Transport and Industry in the immediate post-war period, facilitating a remarkable renaissance after the Japanese occupation. As deputy finance minister in the 1950s, and as finance minister in the 1960s, Cowperthwaite established Hong Kong's unique laissez-faire economic policy. Drawing on Adam Smith, David Ricardo, John Stuart Mill and others, Cowperthwaite crafted twentieth century economic policies consistent with the insights of the classical economists of two centuries earlier. Over a critical twenty-year period, Cowperthwaite argued passionately for his laissez-faire, free-market approach and fought off constant attempts to expand the role of the state.

As two quite different individuals they were the architects of two quite different economies, and in turn two quite distinctive societies. Both viewed economic policy as part of a broader responsibility to shape how we live and work. Both were questioning how to create a better civilization here on Earth, using the tools that they had. Since they were united in their question but so divergent in their answer, they are arguably the originators of the most significant natural economic experiment of the last century.

Although Guevara left Cuba for the last time in 1966, and Cowperthwaite retired in 1971, their economic philosophies have directly influenced economic policy for Cuba and Hong Kong over the last half century. Despite pressures to the contrary,

Hong Kong has maintained its laissez-faire, low tax, private ownership, open economy model virtually unchanged. Cuba has retained the Marxist state-ownership, centrally planned model, and although it has periodically adopted a more Soviet approach, it has always returned to the Guevarist focus on alienation, people, education and healthcare. Guevara's human orientation can perhaps explain why Cuba has remained communist when virtually every other such regime has crumpled.

In the 1950s the two economies produced similar levels of income per capita. It would have been a brave person who would claim with any confidence that Hong Kong would go on to outpace Cuba. Cuba had been successful for centuries, was well located, rich in natural resources and had shaken off Spanish colonialism. Hong Kong was cramped, lacked even adequate water, was unable to feed itself and had an increasingly anachronistic and insecure political structure.

Cuba also seemed to be more in tune with the leading economic beliefs of the day. Post-war, the centre of economic philosophy had decisively shifted to the belief that governments should take responsibility for growth, employment and efficiency rather than leaving that to the market. The developed West largely accepted that the extension of the state seen after the Great Depression and World War II was here to stay. Beveridge thought that Britain would need to move 'half-way to Moscow' to ensure full employment (Timmins 2006). And Keynes agreed that 'Russian methods' might well be necessary (Tombs 2014). There was a fear that the Soviet Union in particular was on a faster development path that would allow it to surpass the capitalist West.

We now know that the Soviet system was much weaker than was assumed in the 1960s and 70s. Their growth was partly driven by huge and poorly directed investment at the expense of consumption, by shifting agricultural workers to industry and by simple fabrication. But many economists in the West were duped into overestimating the success of communist systems (Levy and Peart 2009). The 1961 edition of Nobel-winning economist Paul Samuelson's ubiquitous textbook predicted that the Soviet national income would overtake that of the US possibly by 1984, and probably by 1997 (Samuelson 1961). In the 1989 edition, published shortly before the collapse of the USSR, Samuelson stated that 'the Soviet economy is proof that, contrary to what many sceptics had earlier believed, a socialist command economy can function and prosper' (Samuelson 1989).

The Western developed world embraced the Keynesian revolution, greatly extending the role of the government in the economy. Governments were now expected to actively manage macroeconomic policies, interest rates and fiscal policy to ensure full employment; to develop industrial plans and select favoured industries, using nationalization and regulation to create competitive businesses; manage exchange rates and trade policy to create international competitiveness; set higher taxation, increase state spending and redistribute to deliver greater equality; and generally to intervene actively rather than to stand back and allow markets to resolve issues.

How much of this policy prescription did Hong Kong adopt? Virtually nothing. Instead, the Hong Kong government eschewed the idea of industrial planning, or picking winners, and instead let the market decide which firms prospered and which perished. Rather than run deficits, they aimed for surpluses to provide a reserve equivalent to a year's spending. Instead of protecting chosen industries, or using exchange controls to manage trade flows, they permitted free movement of goods, services and capital. And taxation was kept low in the belief that private investment would create high returns and expand the long-term tax base.

Just as capitalism had a number of variants, so too did socialism. From its earliest days, after the Russian civil war of 1917–1922, there was a debate as to how far to take collectivization and nationalization,* and how much to rely on 'capitalist' tools such as prices and incentives. Initial policy was complete nationalization and an abolition of capitalist mechanisms. But this undermined any incentive to produce in this predominately agricultural economy and so output collapsed. Lenin's New Economic Policy introduced in 1921 permitted greater private ownership of small farms, reintroduced incentives to produce and allowed profits to be earnt and retained. Even Lenin accepted that this step back reintroduced an element of capitalism, described as 'state capitalism', which he expected to remain in place for some decades. But when Stalin ordered aggressive and rapid industrialization in 1928, he dropped the New Economic Plan and reverted to extensive collectivization, nationalization and a controlling five-year plan. This brutal policy had some success at delivering industrialization and reducing unemployment. It would become Soviet orthodoxy as to how to develop when other countries entered the Soviet sphere.

How far to nationalize businesses, and how much to use prices and incentives, would become a contentious debate in Cuba, with policy swinging back and forth over the years. Cuba would go further than most in its policies of state ownership and con-

---

* Collectivization is the process of forcing small farms to consolidate into a larger collective enterprise, which may be collectively or state owned. Nationalization involves the state taking ownership of business enterprises, either with or without compensation.

trol. There was a strong belief that widespread planning could eliminate the vagaries of the market. Idle capacity could be put to use. The optimal quantities of each item could be manufactured, eliminating shortages and surpluses and their associated price fluctuations. Rather than being run for the benefit of a small elite, the economy could be optimized to benefit society as a whole. And instead of companies haphazardly investing in fragmented opportunities, the state could direct investment in a coordinated and strategic way.

This was an economic approach that had little in common with Hong Kong's privately owned, free-market, laissez-faire approach. The divergence between Cuba's and Hong Kong's economic policies over the last half century is only matched by the disparity of their economic performance. The difference is clear from the moment you arrive at their respective main airports. Chek Lap Kok handles 75 million passengers annually through one of the most advanced airports in the world.[1] Havana's José Marti's 5.7 million passengers are left in no doubt that they are using a developing world airport.[2]

The drive from airport to town centre could not be more different. The towering blocks of Hong Kong, the vast port facilities and the brightly lit skyline of downtown Hong Kong contrast with the shanty towns you pass in Cuba before arriving in the bustling but run-down centre of Havana. Hong Kong's buildings are ever more gleaming, prestigious and tall. Over 1,500 skyscrapers stretch more than 100 metres skywards, and there is constant competition to build higher and better.[3] In 2010 the 484-metre International Commerce Centre surpassed the 2003-built Two International Finance Centre's more modest 416 metres. By contrast, Havana's tallest building is the 121-metre-high FOSCA building.[4] It was built between 1954 and 1956 prior to the Cuban Revolution, as were the only other two buildings in Havana taller than 100 metres.

From a distance, the stylish buildings in Havana look grand and impressive. But up close, behind the facades, they are often crumbling and decrepit. Many areas are reminiscent of a bombed-out warzone. The buildings, clearly notable in their day, have been left to crumble over the last few decades. Despite their dilapidated state, each building is packed with residents. Families have sectioned off areas to call their own, including hallways, roofs and every nook and cranny. Where floors had high ceilings, they have been divided laterally by a mezzanine level to create an upper and a lower level.

In Hong Kong, amongst all the wealth and prosperity of that society, you occasionally come across a memento of older, less developed times, reminding you that Hong Kong was not always as wealthy as it is now. In Cuba you can see, on almost every street, signs of the older, grander past, reminding you that Cuba was not always as comparatively poor as it is today. One society has seen remarkable development over the last few decades, the other economic stagnation.

The data on income levels per capita paints the same picture. Cuba and Hong Kong had very similar levels of GDP per capita in the 1950s, at around $4,600–$4,700 per person in today's money.[5] This was around a third of that enjoyed by the UK at that time (or a bit less than a quarter of the US). By the time Hong Kong was reunited with China in 1997, Hong Kong had grown to have the same income per capita as Britain. Today it has an income per capita of around $64,000. That is 40% higher than Britain, and the same as that of the US and Switzerland. Cuba, by contrast, has an income per capita of approximately

$9,000 today. On this measure Cuba is twice as prosperous as it was in the 1950s, while Hong Kong is fourteen times richer. In two generations Hong Kong has moved from being one of the poorest countries in the world to being one of the richest. Over that same period Cuba has moved from being one of the richest countries in Latin America to being one of the poorest.[*]

Importantly, Hong Kong has continued to prosper even after surpassing the affluence of countries such as Britain, France and Germany. It has not only caught up but now outstripped most Western economies. Given that remarkable performance, it is surprising how little attention is paid by economists and politicians to how Hong Kong has created such prosperity. And it is equally surprising that more attention is not paid to understanding how that prosperity has eluded Cuba.

Now is an appropriate time to review the performance of the two economies. We can assess how well 60 years of stable economic policy have translated into long-term prosperity. Hong Kong has followed Cowperthwaite's policy mix since he held office. And Cuba has always returned to the humanist approach promoted by Guevara, with heavy spending on education, healthcare and the reduction of alienation, even though it has experimented with other forms of communism, especially the Soviet approach.

But now change is the air. Hong Kong faces a challenge to the political settlement with Beijing, which runs the risk of affecting the economy of Hong Kong. In Cuba there have been tentative steps towards increased economic liberalization and greater

---

[*] South America is the geographical area on the American continent south of the Panama isthmus. Latin America includes all American and Caribbean countries that speak Romance languages.

openness to the world. The multi-decade experiment of pitting the economic policies of free-market capitalism against those of state communism may be coming to an end. If so, it will be important not to lose the insights of this notable period. And if either economy diverges from its well-worn path, a second experiment will emerge, highlighting how those changes affect future prosperity.

As far as we know, Guevara and Cowperthwaite never met. However, in 1959 Che Guevara visited Hong Kong just after he and Castro had just come to power in Cuba. He was touring a number of countries to consider what type of economic policy the new Cuban government should adopt (Álvarez de Toledo 2010). He found little that inspired him in Hong Kong, other than trying to purchase a camera duty-free. He would return to Cuba more influenced by his meeting with Chairman Mao in Beijing and with President Tito in Yugoslavia. It would be fascinating to get Cowperthwaite and Guevara's perspectives on the story of these two economies. We know that Cowperthwaite was proud of what he had helped Hong Kong to achieve, but he was reticent to discuss his contribution after he had retired, and he died in 2006. Guevara died in Bolivia less than a decade after the Cuban revolution. His writings and speeches were mostly produced in the optimistic post-revolution period. As economic success proved more difficult to deliver, he became more reticent, and eventually returned to guerrilla warfare in Congo and then Bolivia. Maybe he would have been disappointed by the performance of the Cuban economy but more satisfied that much of his philosophy is still alive in Cuba today.

The purpose of this book is to explore these two contrasting economic journeys. Both stories present any researcher with challenges, particularly around the income data for reasons that will be discussed later in the book. But, given the huge difference in outcome, the distinctiveness of their economic policies and the consistency of those policies over decades, small differences in data do not impinge on the key questions raised by this comparison.

> How did Hong Kong become so prosperous? Why did Cuba stagnate economically for so long?
>
> Could Hong Kong have ended up poor or Cuba have ended up rich? What would it have taken to reverse the outcome?

This book explores how humans deliver economic prosperity. The key actors in the story are the people who determine economic policy, in a complicated and unclear environment, with competing aims and preferences, with their specific biases, knowledge and experience. It is a study of them and the extent to which they succeed. Over the 20th century, economics drifted away from the broad canvas introduced by Adam Smith in an attempt to become more scientific. However, the desire to add rigour and professionalism came at a hidden cost (Backhouse 2002). The objective of economics was changed into a technocratic one of optimizing ends given scarce means. The actors became economists rather than policymakers.

 Science requires that identical experiments produce identical results but, once people are involved, all sorts of variation occurs in practice. This story accepts that messiness. In so doing new hypotheses emerge, such as the role of individuals, the role of human capital, the exceptions that are made and the like. One of the premises of the book is that 'we are pattern-seeking, story-telling animals'[6] and therefore if the objective is to improve economic policy makers' decisions, then a good way to do that is to search for important and significant patterns, and to express them in a narrative form.

The first chapter presents the critical decision point faced by Hong Kong and Cuba in the late 1950s and early 1960s. They were both required to make some fundamental choices about what future economic policies they wanted to adopt. Chapter Two explores the economic and political context of those debates. Chapter Three delves into the two main protagonists, Cowperthwaite and Guevara, to consider how their backgrounds and experiences shaped their economic views. These two men would be critical in answering the question of economic direction. Chapter Four explains the world views and economic philosophies that Guevara and Cowperthwaite developed and relied upon. As far as possible this chapter uses their own words to describe their views; they were both very articulate, and the use of their style and logic gives a useful sense of the two individuals. Chapters Five and Six summarize the actual policies, organization and decisions that have been made in Cuba and Hong Kong since the 1960s, based on their framework. Chapter Seven highlights the results that Hong Kong and Cuba have produced over the last 60 years or so. Lastly, Chapter Eight attempts to draw some lessons, or at least to propose some hypotheses about what we can learn from the story of Hong Kong and Cuba: of Ernesto 'Che' Guevara and Sir John James Cowperthwaite.

THE CHOICE

The 1960s ushered in a period of great change across the world. Many old certainties dissolved with the conclusion of post-war reconstruction and the breakdown of the pre-war social order. Things that had seemed impossible a few years earlier suddenly became achievable. The combination of new social norms, and the surge in technologies such as transistors, plastics, television and mass production generated new opportunities. The resultant change was clearly manifest in culture, music, television, film and fashion. But it was also evident in the anti-war, civil rights and anti-colonialism protests that demanded change. And within the constraints of the rift of the cold war, national politics was also changing. After the horrors of World War II, and the subsequent struggle to rebuild basic infrastructure, people could look forward and think about the world that they would like to shape.

Economic policy was a part of that debate. The great divide was between capitalism and the communism,* exemplified by the

---

* Socialism and Communism are broad and overlapping terms. Socialism tries to reduce the inequality that it ascribes to capitalism, especially via state control

United States and the Soviet Union. However, neither country was a particularly faithful example of its philosophy. From Hong Kong's perspective the United States and many Western countries appeared to have a large and expanding activist state, high taxation, interference in trade and a reckless approach to government finances. From Cuba's perspective it looked as though the USSR was using the tools of capitalist economics to build socialism, with a vast network of controls, plans, incentives and rewards regularly used to encourage individuals to give 'from each according to his ability'.

Hong Kong and Cuba would reject the emerging orthodoxy of a mixed economy with widespread government activism and involvement, designed to balance the interests of capital, labour and the state. Instead, they would hark back to a purer form of their respective models. Cuba would look to Karl Marx, and Hong Kong to Adam Smith. It would fall to Guevara and Cowperthwaite to lay the foundations of their economies and their societies.

THE HONG KONG QUESTION

Hong Kong had recovered surprisingly rapidly after the Japanese occupation during World War II (Donnison 1956). With no funds available from war-torn Britain, it had been a self-engi-

---

and ownership. Communism is the stage after socialism, where work is unalienated and goods and services are universally available. Cuba is in a socialist phase. In this book, economies that are aiming to become Marxist communist states, as opposed to just redistributing wealth within a capitalist system, are called communist.

neered recovery, relying on the business sector to seize opportunities. It had nearly all unravelled when the entrepôt* trade with China virtually disappeared after the United States imposed sanctions on trading with China during the Korean War.

Figure 1. Nanyang cotton spinning mill in Hong Kong (1963)

Fortunately, Hong Kong businesses had been developing an industrial capability, especially around textiles (Riedel 1974). This had been bolstered when some leading Chinese textile entrepreneurs relocated to Hong Kong after the communist victory in China. As the entrepôt trade died, textile investments and output grew, and by 1960 textiles had become a sizeable part of the Hong Kong economy. But this had brought unanticipated problems as the US and the UK in particular railed against the surge in cheap textile imports from Hong Kong. The US and UK had

---

* An entrepôt is a port or city where goods are imported and then stored and traded, usually to be exported again.

sizeable, inefficient, high-cost textile sectors, located in politically important regions, and so the boom in Hong Kong's textile industry was the mirror image of the decline in their textile sectors, with the inevitable impact on jobs.

Whilst the US and the UK both argued for the benefits of free trade in general, they were a lot less enthusiastic about how Hong Kong's textile exporters were, in practice, decimating their domestic industry. Under GATT (the General Agreement on Tariffs and Trade) they were in theory limited in their ability to raise protectionist barriers, and yet they did all they could to threaten and cajole Hong Kong into enforcing an 'orderly market'.

The UK government, led by Harold Macmillan, wanted to protect domestic manufacturing, especially in Lancashire, the centre of the UK cotton industry. Hong Kong was pressured to sign up to the Lancashire Agreement, which would 'voluntarily' limit exports to the UK. Pressure from the US increased dramatically during the presidential election of 1960. When President Kennedy took office, he was himself under pressure to make good on his campaign promises and to help the textile industry.

There were a few who argued in favour of free trade, a rare example being a 1961 editorial in the *New York Times*.[7]

> President Kennedy's program for assistance to the textile industry implies that he is seriously thinking of imposing quotas on textile imports into this country. If any such quotas are set he will have made a serious error bowing to political pressure which he should have withstood. The imposition of textile import quotas would... contradict this country's long and ardent advocacy of the freest possible international trade.

But the mood was mostly protectionist. In the US and the UK some amazing theories were being peddled about Hong Kong's cost advantage, including that the companies were deeply loss-making, or that they had large government subsidies. The truth was more difficult to deal with: Hong Kong manufacturers had labour cost advantages, more modern machinery and better asset utilization. In a sign of the prevailing mood, in May 1962 *The Economist* called the Hong Kong textile operators 'buccaneers', arguing that 'whenever some semblance of an orderly trading arrangement for general advantage looms in Hong Kong, it is trampled to bits by rampaging freebooters'.[8]

In early 1960 it was against this background that the then financial secretary,* Arthur Clarke, introduced his budget. He was in a sombre mood. He had presided over eight years of growth as financial secretary but could see that government expenditure would rise in the years ahead as the government spent more on housing, education and other services. He was doubtful that revenues could grow as rapidly as needed whilst overseas markets erected tariff barriers against Hong Kong exports (Monnery 2017). He warned:

> We have, I think, come to a turning point in our financial history. [Reserves] will carry us through next year, but what then? Are we to go on running deficits each year and running down our reserves until there is nothing left? Are we to borrow on the best terms we can? Or are we to step up the rate of tax?[9]

---

* The finance minister in Hong Kong is called financial secretary and reports directly to the governor on economic matters. It is a role with considerable power and independence.

He went on to broaden the question beyond the financial one:

> There seem to be two courses we can follow. We can carry on as we are doing. We can continue to allow our industry to expand; to continue to increase our exports to promising markets year by year, with our manufacturers competing against each other, cutting their prices, cutting their profit margins, until those markets are closed, or partially closed, to us, with the disruption to our economy that must follow.
>
> Or we can do something to plan our economy. We can see to it that for the future we do not advance past the point where markets have to be closed to us because we are selling too much, too quickly, too cheaply. This means that we would have to abandon our traditional policy of laissez-faire at least as far as exports are concerned. We would have to guide and direct; we would have to regulate and control. Which course should we adopt?[10]

The members of the Legislative Council* were struck by the importance of the question that Clarke was posing, and shared Clarke's view that it was a question that now needed to be addressed. One member spoke for many when he noted:

> There is, of course, no simple solution to this problem. While I am afraid that the policy of complete 'laissez-faire' which served us so well in the fifties might well lead us to economic disaster in the 60's, I would be reluctant to advocate a sudden switch to the regulations and controls that are the price to be paid for a highly planned economy.[11]

---

* The Legislative Council passed legislation for Hong Kong. It comprised a majority of executive officials, and a number of 'unofficial' members, appointed by the governor and intended to represent business and the community.

Like all good politicians, he wondered if there was:

> a middle way… a path well clear of the dangerous abyss into which the 'laissez-faire' route might lead us, but clear also of the throttling jungle of too many controls. [A] middle path of guidance from both Government and the Banks should lead us to the diversification of our industries (and the) Government might assist the situation by adopting Pioneer Industry techniques.[12]

Clarke did not push the debate to reach any conclusions. He was retiring the following year and knew that it would be for his successor, Cowperthwaite, to decide to how to proceed. He was happy to have posed the vital question, so that Cowperthwaite could explicitly choose how to spend his time in office, and how he could best enable Hong Kong to prosper in the years ahead. His remarks were well received in London, where the Treasury, Colonial Office and key politicians had long disliked the way that Hong Kong economic policy had diverged so far away from that of the UK. Cowperthwaite stayed silent, waiting until he was in office to make his views clear.

THE CUBAN QUESTION

In the early hours of the morning of 1 January 1959 Fulgencio Batista, the authoritarian president of Cuba, fled to the Dominican Republic with various friends, supporters and an estimated $700 million in cash, art and bullion. The day before, the town of Santa Clara had fallen to the rebels led by Fidel Castro. This defeat left the two main insurgent armies within easy reach of Havana. During the night of 2 January Che Guevara's column arrived in the northern part of Havana to take control of the barracks at La Cabaña, and Camilo Cienfuegos's column arrived to take over the barracks at Camp Columbia in western Havana. The rebels had won, and Castro's two key military lieutenants were in charge of the capital's two strategic military barracks (Álvarez de Toledo 2010).

Castro slowly made his way from Santa Clara to Havana, receiving the support of hundreds of thousands who turned out to see him and to show their approval at the ending of the Batista regime. It had been a popular uprising with a variety of movements cooperating to bring down Batista. They had been united in that aim, but it was unclear how the coalition would develop broader policies. Castro had emerged as the leader of the armed revolution, but there were others who had played a military or political role. And Castro had been careful not to be too explicit about what he thought should happen after the overthrow of Batista. He had needed not only a broad base of supporters in Cuba but also the tacit support of the United States, and he had been careful not to alienate them.

Castro had outlined his most detailed economic manifesto prior to taking office six years earlier, in 1953, when he was tried for a previous attack on the state (Szulc 1986). In his four-hour defence summing up (later titled: 'History will absolve me') he proposed five revolutionary laws that would be enacted immediately the revolution occurred. These were: to return power to the people and reinstate the constitution of 1940; to gift all smallholdings to those working the land and to compensate owners by paying them ten years of rent; to give workers in large commercial concerns the right to 30% of their profits; to give sugar producers the right to 55% of the profits of production; and to confiscate the property of those found guilty of corruption or fraud and to earmark this money for workers' pensions and for healthcare (Gott 2004). These five measures would be followed by nationalized public utilities and reorganized public education, and required the government to find or offer employment to the unemployed.

Between 1953 and 1959 Castro continued to highlight reform, equity and nationalism rather than a communist agenda. He focused his message on overthrowing Batista and reiterating his demand for land reform, broader education and healthcare. This package of aspirations allowed for cohesion between the anti-Batista movements, and even the communist party was not agitating for a Marxist solution at that time.

Castro orchestrated the appointment of Manuel Urrutia Lleó as president and José Miró Cardona as prime minister (Gott 2004). Cardona had been one of Castro's professors and, like Urrutia, was a liberal lawyer. Castro himself took on the role of head of the army and military commander-in-chief. It would not be long before he would assume much greater power, but for now he allowed the new cabinet some latitude. Meanwhile the revolutionary commanders formalized their personal relations, with Raúl Castro marrying Vilma Espin, an engineer and the daughter of a wealthy lawyer, and in January 1959 Guevara divorced his first wife to marry Aleida March, who had been an active fighter under his command (Anderson 1997).

Figure 2. Guevara, Castro, Manuel Urrutia and Camilo Cienfuegos, Havana 1959

The leaders of the revolutionary army were preoccupied with preventing a counter-revolution, as they had seen happen elsewhere. To that end, hundreds of Batista supporters were summarily tried and executed. Some televised trials took place in the sports stadium, with the crowd baying for justice. Others were executed in private. Raúl Castro, who had become the military commander in Oriente, signed many death warrants, and was alleged to have organized mass killings where Batista soldiers were machine gunned in front of burial trenches. Guevara, as the commander of La Cabaña, confirmed at least 50 death sentences, arguing (Werlau 2011):

> We executed many people by firing squad without knowing if they were fully guilty. At times, the Revolution cannot stop to conduct much investigation; it has the obligation to triumph.

Whilst the revolutionaries were busy eliminating opponents and settling old scores, Urrutia focused the government's energy on some of his pet projects, closing casinos, brothels and the national lottery. The property and assets of Batista and his friends were seized. In March 1959 Guevara suffered very severe asthma and needed to spend several months recuperating on the coast at Tararà, to the east of Havana (Álvarez de Toledo 2010). Much of the government would travel back and forth to meet with him, and Castro asked him to use the time to create a new state security system, develop economic policies and design Cuba's diplomatic stance vis-à-vis the rest of South America (Gonzalez 2004).

The revolutionary members of the government realized that they would need to take more radical actions than the liberal government were likely to initiate themselves. More significantly, policies were adopted to reduce rents, ban the eviction of tenants and limit the prices charged for telephone and energy services. In April a minimum wage was introduced for sugar cane cutters. But Castro was increasingly aware that he needed to make good on his promise of land reform, and that meant taking on the liberals and the US landowners.

Castro again used Guevara as a driver of change. In January 1959 Guevara made an important speech arguing for 'the social justice that land reform brings about', and he worked on drafting a new Agrarian Reform Law. In a speech in the Sierra Maestra in May 1959, Castro described how land reform would work. For any estates above 1,000 acres the excess would be subject to seizure. There were exceptions for very productive plantations and for cattle ranches, and there would be compensation for the land seized. Even so, it was estimated that 40% of farmland would be appropriated and would be broken up into 67-acre plots for individuals to farm or to be run as cooperatives. One measure that would cause great concern in the United States was that only Cubans would be able to own land, and so the large contingent of US landowners would be forced to sell.

The new statute came into force on 17 May 1959. The entire cabinet was required to sign the law, but the very divergent agendas were not easily disguised by an artificial act of solidarity. Castro could see that his careful blend of being anti-Batista, anti-crony capitalism, pro-nationalism and pro-reform would soon run out of road.

But even as late as July 1959, Castro would assert:

> I am not a communist and neither is the revolutionary movement.[13]

But, being a skilled politician, he knew that he could not afford to leave a vacuum once land reform had bedded down. He would need to decide between the liberals and the old (landed) elite – who felt that there was too much change, and who increasingly looked to the United States to help slow that – and the communists, such as his brother Raúl and Guevara, who wanted reforms to go much further, and were looking towards Soviet Russia and Maoist China for the way forward. Castro needed an agenda and a mechanism to deliver it. And he increasingly understood that he might need a powerful ally should the US turn hostile.

To implement land reform, a new department was established, the National Institute for Agrarian Reform (INRA). This would be led by Castro and would emerge as the real headquarters of the revolutionary government (Gott 2004). It would give Castro a way to circumvent the normal departments of state, or simply to absorb them into .INRA.

As for what to do, Castro once more turned to Guevara, who had recovered and returned to Havana. In June 1959 Castro asked him to embark on a three-month world tour of various economies to help gather information on what Cuba should do (Anderson 1997). At first, Guevara was concerned that he was being side-lined and would be absent in the critical formative months of the new government, but he would soon realize that he was to be the key architect of the Cuban economic system. He would end up running the department of industry within INRA with a very broad remit, he would head the central bank, sit on the Council of Ministers and be the chief negotiator with the Soviet bloc. With these platforms he would hold primary responsibility for charting the direction of Cuba's economic policies for generations to come.

Just as the debate was structured in Hong Kong, Guevara described two alternative approaches to running an economy, the first of which combined laissez-faire, capitalism and private ownership:

> How to develop our economy, by what means? There are two ways. One is called the free enterprise way. It used to be expressed by a French phrase which means 'let be'. All economic forces, supposedly on an equal footing, would freely compete with each other and bring about the country's development. That is what we had in Cuba and what did it get us? It showed how deeply a people can enslave itself by economic means, without realizing it in the slightest.[14]

Guevara noted that in Cuba there had been a dictatorship, and widespread crony capitalism, but for him it was the free market system that was the core problem, and he argued that 'all this could have been done without any dictatorship'. Guevara believed that there was an alternative that could overcome these defects:

> But there is another system. It is the system in which we face up to ourselves and tell ourselves, 'we are revolutionaries, the revolutionary government, the people's representatives'. And who do we have to make these industries for, if not the people? If the people must benefit, and we are the people's representatives, we, the government, should carry the weight and the direction of industrialization, so there will not be any anarchy.

Everything and everyone were now in place for Hong Kong and Cuba to embark on their unique economic paths: paths to which they would remain broadly true for the subsequent 60 years. Given the distinctiveness and longevity of their policies, these countries provide a remarkable natural experiment as to how economic policies affect prosperity.

NATURAL EXPERIMENTS

Economists sometimes lament that it is impossible to conduct macroeconomic experiments in the same way as in, say, chemistry or physics. Strong, predictive stable relationships between pulling one economic policy lever and delivering a precise economic output are elusive. The complexity of cause and effect results in economists often caveating their policy recommendations, as illustrated by Ronald Regan's famous request that the White House recruit a one-armed economist, who would, he thought, avoid saying 'on the one hand…, but on the other…'.

Ideally, it would be possible to take two identical economies that, without intervention, would perform identically, then vary one input, say taxation rates, and assess the effect. But even that would be illusory because economic effects will vary according to what other changes are being made and as the situation changes. The combined influence of investment levels, of the rule of law, of political institutions, of property rights, of productivity, of education levels, of health, of the quality of management, of openness to trade, of exchange rate policy, of fiscal policy, of monetary policy and so on would need to be understood. If they interacted (which they surely do) and if their impact varies according to the situation (as it surely must), then the difficulty in understanding the complexity of causes and effects in complicated systems such as economies is clear.

What is possible, however, is to find naturally occurring situations, analyse what does occur in the real world and try to tease apart cause and effect, significance and triviality, universality and uniqueness. As Milton Friedman observed (Friedman 1953):

Unfortunately, we can seldom test particular predictions in the social sciences by experiments explicitly designed to eliminate what are judged to be the most important disturbing influences. Generally, we must rely on evidence cast by the 'experiments' that happen to occur.

Rather than a control group, isolated inputs and outputs, we can instead look to 'the stream of experiments that nature is steadily turning out from her own enormous laboratory, and which we merely watch as passive observers' (Haavelmo 1944).

One of the earliest natural experiments concerned the spread of disease rather than economics. In 1854 an outbreak of cholera in Soho, London, was analysed by doctor John Snow (Snow 1855). Over a two-month period over 600 people died and Snow was unconvinced by the contemporary claim that cholera was caused by airborne particles coming from decaying or dirty organic matter. Without the benefit of technology or an understanding of microbiology, he nonetheless correctly concluded that the disease was transmitted by germ-infected water. He came to this view by plotting victims' locations on a map and interviewing them or their families, and also those not infected. He observed that all those infected had drunk water from the public water pump on Broad Street, whereas those who did not use that pump, either because they were further away or drank only beer or other alcohol, did not. His investigations revealed that the source for that pump was a part of the River Thames that had significant sewage contamination.

There has been some analysis of natural experiments in the macroeconomic field. Perhaps there should be more, given the difficulty of 'scientific' experiments in macroeconomics. For example, Friedman used three episodes of US economic history to explore the causes of the Great Depression (Friedman 2006). Reviewing that, Ben Bernanke argued that (Bernanke 2002):

> The special genius of the Monetary History is the authors' use of what some today would call 'natural experiments' – episodes in which money moves for reasons that are plausibly unrelated to the current state of the economy.

Bernanke argued that these natural experiments did implicate monetary policy as a cause of the Great Depression. He also noted how such analysis can be incorporated in economics:

> Of course, natural experiments are never perfectly controlled, so that no single natural experiment can be viewed as dispositive – hence the importance of Friedman and Schwartz's historical analysis, which adduces a wide variety of such episodes and comparisons in support of their case.

There has been some use of natural experiments in understanding the drivers of economic growth. Acemoglu *et al.* (2005) contrasted the economic success of a number of adjacent territories that ended up with different institutions, for example, contrasting South Korea. with North Korea. They argued that the two economies shared history, people, culture, geography and the like, and so revealed the importance of economic institutions in determining economic development. Other similar pairings are East and West Germany, and North and South Vietnam. Or economies can be examined across different time periods, such as Eastern Europe under communism and after the fall of communism. The unique element of the Cuba–Hong Kong experiment is that they chose very distinct economic policies, far from the mainstream mixed-economy formula. And rather than switching back and forth between economic policies, they have held their economic policies broadly stable for a very long time.

THE END OF THIS EXPERIMENT?

Given the changes that may be happening in Hong Kong and Cuba today, now is an apposite time to review this natural experiment. In both economies, change may be in the wind, and the stability of historical policy measures may be coming to an end.

When Hong Kong was returned to China in 1997, China agreed that the Hong Kong economic system should retain its essential character for at least 50 years after reunification. China asserted its sovereignty over Hong Kong, but agreed that it would allow 'one country, two systems'. China agreed to the Hong Kong Basic Law, which provides a constitutional framework for how Hong Kong should be run during this period. In the agreement, Hong Kong was established as a Special Administrative Region of China, but:

> The socialist system and policies shall not be practiced in the Hong Kong Special Administrative Region, and the previous capitalist system and way of life shall remain unchanged for 50 years. (Chapter 1, article 5)

At a more specific level, several clauses protect Hong Kong's right to retain free trade, and to remain a business-friendly setting for international finance and trade. Article 107 guarantees financial prudence and limits the size and growth of government spending. Article 108 safeguards Hong Kong's low tax approach in future policy decisions. In many ways, the early years of reunification saw most of the distinct approach taken by Hong Kong carrying on with little change. To many it seemed that the 'one country, two systems' approach could succeed (Carroll 2007). In economic policy the budgets produced by recent financial secretaries could have been written by earlier incumbents.

More recently, there have been increasing doubts that China will allow as much autonomy as existed before and that many believe is built into the Basic Law. In 2014 the 'umbrella revolution' saw protests against China's move to have more control over who sat on the Legislative Council. In 2015 five booksellers who had stocked books critical of China and its leaders disappeared, with some being abducted to mainland China.[15] Various opposition politicians have claimed that their freedoms have been impinged. In 2019, mass protests broke out as China attempted to impose an extradition law. There are signs that these conflicts around political and individual rights may start to infringe on Hong Kong's economic model. There is a widespread concern as to the future for the rule of law, property rights and the non-political nature of the administration of the territory.

Should Hong Kong have the misfortune to lose its economic momentum, it will be a tragedy for the its people. It would, however, be a valuable natural economic experiment. What can drive an economy that has been successful for more than half a century into reverse gear? What would bring this great journey of prosperity to an end?

And change is also in the air in Cuba. Modest reforms were made in the early 1990s, allowing some foreign investment, some tolerance of limited self-employment and some expansion of the banking system. In 2014 Presidents Barack Obama and Raúl Castro agreed to the 'Cuban Thaw', whereby there would be some normalization of US-Cuban relations. With the death of Fidel Castro in 2016 and the retirement of Raúl Castro in 2018, it looked as if Cuba would be evolving its historical approach. President Donald Trump reversed some of these changes, making the future less clear. But the prospect of Cuba becoming more open to the world and opting for domestic reform remains real, and if Cuba does move away from its Marxist approach, it will be fascinating to see which elements of the model most improve the standard of living of its people. Just as Hong Kong may show what the key elements are that turn prosperity into stagnation, Cuba may reveal what elements turn stagnation into prosperity.

TWO SITUATIONS

Was there something about the two economies that made it inevitable that Cuba would chose Marxism, and Hong Kong free market capitalism? That Hong Kong would prosper, and Cuba stagnate? Could both could have taken the path chosen by the other with the same economic results? Could 1950s Cuba have turned into the economic beacon of Latin America, and could Hong Kong have become the backwater of Asia?

The starting position of each in the late 1950s – their geography, their history, their cultures and people, their economic development and the like – informs the choices that they made, and the alternative worlds that could have been.

GEOGRAPHY

Cuba and Hong Kong both sit at a latitude of around 22 or 23 degrees north, just south of the Tropic of Cancer. But in longitude Hong Kong is 114 degrees east, and Cuba 82 degrees west.

Despite being at the same latitude, Cuba is warmer, with a tropical climate, in part due the warm Caribbean current. Hong Kong has a humid subtropical climate with hot summers and mild winters. Both sit on the path of tropical cyclones, called typhoons in Hong Kong and hurricanes in Cuba, which can cause severe disruption, damage and fatalities. Both lie near potentially important trade routes. Hong Kong is situated at the mouth of the Pearl River, adjacent to the South China Sea. Cuba is strategically placed between the Caribbean and the routes north to the United States and east to Europe.

Perhaps the biggest geographical difference is in land area. Hong Kong has 1,100 square kilometres of hilly terrain, with little arable land and few sources of fresh water. Cuba has over 100,000 square kilometres of mostly flat plains, suitable for agricultural use. Not surprisingly, this difference made it possible for Cuba to develop an agricultural economy where Hong Kong could not, and in the pre-industrial period this led to a level of development in Cuba that greatly surpassed that of Hong Kong. However, Hong Kong has overcome land scarcity in the modern era, and Cuba's vastly superior land resources have not translated into greater overall prosperity.

Hong Kong has almost no natural resources beyond some rock to quarry and some sand to dredge. It is even deficient in water and has had to build reservoirs and, at times, even to import water. Almost all raw materials must be imported. By contrast Cuba has the second largest nickel reserves in the world after Russia, is the fifth largest producer of refined cobalt in the world and has reserves of oil, iron ore and copper. It has rich supplies of timber, including cedar and mahogany, although much of this has been harvested and replanted with sugar cane (Mesa-Lago 1981). Guevara recognized the natural wealth that Cuba enjoyed:

We have a geographical location and an exuberant nature, which allow us an extraordinarily great development. We have unexplored mineral riches. We are for example the world's second largest nickel producer. We have that extraordinary source of wealth, sugar cane, and the capacity to convert all our sugar cane into a chemical sugar industry, which would be a source of inexhaustible wealth.[16]

EARLY HISTORY

Both Hong Kong and Cuba have been inhabited for over 5,000 years, but whereas by the 16th century Cuba had a substantial population numbering over 150,000, the Hong Kong islands were very sparsely populated. Both were discovered by Europeans within twenty years of each other. Christopher Columbus claimed Cuba for Spain in 1492, and Diego Velázquez de Cuéllar founded the first settlement in 1511, and the port of Havana in 1515. A combination of forced labour, violence, measles and smallpox effectively wiped out almost all the indigenous population by the 1530s. Spanish settlers would need to build an economy largely from scratch, albeit on a large, fertile island. With the survivors of the indigenous population, supplemented by some slaves, these settlers slowly built an agricultural base which supplemented the trading role that Havana provided for the Spanish empire (Gott 2004).

Meanwhile Jorge Álvares, the Portuguese explorer, was the first European to visit Hong Kong, in 1513. There was a brief period when Portuguese merchants established a trading post in Hong Kong, but they were expelled in the 1520s. Portugal's interest turned to Macau, and it established a more permanent trading settlement there in 1557. Hong Kong itself drifted back into obscurity.

Over the 17th, 18th and 19th centuries Cuba continued to develop. GDP per capita in today's money rose from a subsistence level of around $500 per capita in 1700 to around $1,300 per capita in 1800 and $3,000 per capita in 1900.[17] This progress was driven by growing trade and agricultural production, especially the expansion of the sugar industry, and later the cigar industry. Hong Kong lagged these levels of prosperity, with a per capita income in 1800 and 1900 similar to that of Cuba's in the 1700s. The Cuban population nearly tripled over the 19th century, to around 1.7 million people, with an influx of slaves to work on the sugar plantations and the arrival of a significant number of Spanish immigrants. The issue of how to treat these slaves and the desire for independence would cause Cubans to rebel against their colonial masters in the late 1800s.

While Cuba developed over three centuries, the same could not be said for Hong Kong. Its lack of resources meant that the population remained small and engaged in local fishing and hunting. In 1662 the new child emperor, Kangxi, even evacuated the coastal area, moving residents inland. It would be the opium trade that would change the fate of Hong Kong. In 1699 the East India Company started trading with China, but it soon became apparent that China's exports to Britain, in particular tea, greatly exceeded Britain's exports to China. With all exports from China being paid for in silver, this drain on British reserves was not acceptable to the mercantilist British.

Britain decided to balance trade flows by importing opium from British-controlled India to be sold in China. Before long Britain had a positive trade balance and China had a drugs epidemic.

The Daoguang Emperor ordered an official, Lin Tse-hsu, to suppress the opium trade, which he did by arresting merchants and destroying opium stocks. Captain Charles Elliot, the British Superintendent of Trade, beat a tactical retreat before returning in 1841 with gunboats and troops to seize Hong Kong. After a further year of fighting on the mainland, the Chinese accepted the Treaty of Nanking, ceding Hong Kong to Britain in perpetuity, opening five Chinese ports to British trade and allowing foreign residents in those ports to be tried by British rather than Chinese courts (Endacott 1964a).

Not everyone was convinced that it was a good thing when Hong Kong became a British possession in 1842. A book on China published in 1847 included a chapter headed 'Hong Kong – its position, prospects, character and utter worthlessness from every point of view to England'. With a population of around 7,000 mostly engaged in fishing and charcoal burning, the island did not look much like an embryonic global trading hub.

COLONIAL HONG KONG, INDEPENDENT CUBA

The second half of the 19th century would see Hong Kong become an established British colony, and Cuba finally achieve its independence from Spain.

A series of wars expanded the Hong Kong colony. The second opium war saw France and Britain join forces, with the support of the United States, to invade China. The war ended with the Treaty of Tientsin in 1858, which opened eleven more Chinese ports and allowed foreigners to trade with China. In 1859 an attempt by the Chinese emperor to beat back the Anglo-French forces failed, and in 1860 the Convention of Peking ceded Kow-loon to Britain. The last expansion of the colony came when Britain exploited Chinese weakness after suffering a defeat from Japan. The second Convention of Peking, in 1898, leased the New Territories to Britain for 99 years, adding 360 square miles of mostly rural land to the colony. With a greater area, and con-siderable immigration, the population reached around 400,000 by 1900, about one-sixth the population of Cuba.

Hong Kong was a small but strategically important part of the British Empire. To the south lay the colonies of Singapore and Malaya, and beyond them Australia and New Zealand. To the west was India, the 'jewel' of the British Empire, and the criti-cally important Middle East and the vital Suez Canal. Hong Kong served two main goals: providing a naval base (although this was less important than the facilities in Singapore) and sup-porting trade.

British commercial activity was predominately concentrated in the trading houses (the Hongs), such as Dent, Russell, Swire and Jardine Matheson. Some, such as Jardine Matheson, became prosperous as opium traders. Niall Ferguson (2003) notes:

> The only real benefit of acquiring Hong Kong as a result of the war of 1841 was that it provided firms like Jardine Mathe-son with a base for their opium-smuggling operation. It is in-deed one of the richer ironies of the Victorian value-system that the same navy that was deployed to abolish the slave trade was also active in expanding the narcotics trade.

The Hongs were increasing their size and breadth, entering new product areas and broadening their interests in China. Their di-versification would serve them well, since in 1907 Britain and China agreed to phase out the opium trade, although that would not be fully achieved until Mao suppressed it in the 1950s by imposing draconian penalties.

The colony was managed by a small cadre of British administrators drawn from the Colonial Office. A governor enjoyed almost absolute control as the representative of the British Crown, supported by key officials. However, one governor, Sir Hercules Robinson, was so unimpressed by the quality of these civil servants that in 1859 he instituted a scheme of competitive examinations to appoint Hong Kong Cadets (Tsang 2007). These select individuals, numbering approximately one appointment per year, would be high-flyers who would learn Chinese and progress rapidly to senior jobs. Only 85 cadets were recruited between 1861 and 1941 (Tsang 2007) and just over 30 were in post by the time of the Japanese occupation. This initiative started to improve the quality of the administration, which would be vital in the 20th century. The progress being made commercially and administratively was not matched by social progress. Society remained socially divided on ethnic and class lines. For many the colony was a small, stifling, incestuous place suited to making money rather than to building a community.

Whilst Hong Kong was becoming established as a British colony, Cuba was moving towards independence. The first major uprising was led by Carlos Manuel de Céspedes, a sugar planter, who in 1868 declared independence from Spain and also freed his slaves to fight with him. The Ten Years' War followed, ending in 1878 with the Pact of Zanjón, which gave Cuba greater autonomy and abolished slavery. But it was not long before the simmering desire for independence would again erupt. However, the Cubans were split between those who wanted independence and those that wanted a continuing link to Spain, as well as on racial lines, as the government successfully split blacks from whites.

In 1895 the fight for full independence resumed. The rebellion was led by the small, neat Jose Martí, who was more of a writer and theorist than warrior. He had been exiled from Cuba in 1871 and again in 1879 for involvement in the independence move-ment and had spent 20 years in New York and Florida as part of the Cuban exiled community (Gott 2004). Martí would become an inspiration to Castro and to many Latin Americans, arguing (Thomas 2001):

> The hands of every nation must remain free, for the untram-
> meled development of the country, in accordance with its dis-
> tinctive nature and with its individual elements.

But he was also at pains to point out that Cuba should not swap the rule of Madrid for that of Washington, warning against be-coming too inter-connected with the US:

> I know the Monster, because I have lived in its lair – and my
> weapon is only the slingshot of David.

Martí believed in a Cuba that united all racial elements and did not try to divide whites from blacks. His was a belief in nation-alism. He landed in Cuba with a small force in early 1895, but within six weeks he had been killed. The uprising would con-tinue without Martí, but his influence would return again in the 1959 revolution.

Spain dispatched a huge army of around 200,000 men to sup-press the uprising, which imprisoned a large part of the civilian population, many of whom died of starvation or disease. The small rebel army relied on guerrilla tactics, but in the end it was the intervention of the United States that would determine the outcome of this war.

The US battleship *USS Maine* was sent to protect US interests but exploded soon after its arrival in Havana harbour, killing the majority of the crew (Franklin 2016). The US blamed Spain for the sinking and in April 1898 President McKinley demanded Spain withdraw from Cuba. He imposed a blockade on Cuba, and Congress declared war on Spain. Given the huge military disparity, the war only lasted for ten weeks and resulted in the inevitable routing of the Spanish forces. In the Treaty of Paris, Spain agreed that Cuba would become independent after a short period of control by the US, and also ceded ownership of Puerto Rico, Guam and the Philippines. It was the end of the Spanish empire that had lasted for five centuries, and the start of the American empire. It also largely completed the objectives of the Monroe Doctrine, which insisted that European powers should disengage from colonialism on the American continent.

Cuba became an independent nation on 20 May 1902 (Franklin 2016). Foreshadowing conflicts ahead, the US retained a role in Cuban affairs. Congress had passed the Platt Amendment, which allowed the US to intervene in the case of domestic political instability, and this plus a role in foreign affairs was incorporated into the new Cuban constitution. It would not be long before the intertwined nature of the two countries was evident. But, as the new century dawned, Cuba was, for the first time in nearly 300 years, free from its colonial past.

HONG KONG AND THE SECOND WORLD WAR

In the first half of the 20th century both Hong Kong and Cuba were to suffer invasions: one from the Japanese, one from the United States. The nature of those occupations would be very different but, in both cases, would leave wounds that would take time to heal. The Japanese occupation of Hong Kong was brutal and destructive and would leave a wasteland for the post-1945 population to rebuild. The US occupation of Cuba would see a deep involvement by the US in Cuban politics and industry. Whilst funds might flow, many would question whether Cuba, and its ruling elites, were working for the Cubans.

Until 1941 Hong Kong had made gradual progress. It continued to grow and develop as an entrepôt during the early 20th century, with economic activity centred around the trade with China, and all the associated support activities. The population reached half a million in the mid-1910s, then three-quarters of a million in the1920s, heading above a million in the 1930s. Even when World War II broke out in 1939, Hong Kong seemed a very long way away from the conflict in Europe.

All that changed on 7 December 1941. On that day Japan attacked Pearl Harbor, but it also attacked Hong Kong, the Philippines, Thailand and Malaya. Britain knew that Hong Kong was not defensible, as Churchill had acknowledged to army commanders a year earlier. He hoped, however, that the defence would be robust. On 10 December the two in-theatre battleships, *HMS Repulse* and *HMS Prince of Wales* were sunk off Malaya. Without sea power, and with only five (obsolete) aircraft, the approach to Hong Kong lay undefended, and by 18 December the Japanese had landed on Hong Kong island. The speed and ferocity of the Japanese advance made defeat inevitable.

Knowing that the Japanese had also massacred wounded hospital patients and medical staff, the governor chose to surrender on 25 December, to limit further casualties from combat and war crimes (Tsang 2004).

The Japanese occupation would be a dark period in Hong Kong's history. Around 11,000 people, comprising Commonwealth forces, Hong Kong's civil servants and any remaining expatriates, were interned in several prisoner-of-war camps. The local population was subject to torture and oppression, and almost all property was looted or seized. Any assets in factories, offices and the port that could be taken were. The four years of occupation would see the economy collapse and the population fall from around 1.5 million before the war, to around 600,000.

In the early morning of 6 August 1945, the *Enola Gay* dropped 'Little Boy' on Hiroshima. Tens of thousands died that day, and many more from radiation poising over the subsequent weeks. Three days later, *Bockscar* dropped a second atomic bomb, 'Fat Man', on Nagasaki, causing similar casualties. Japan surrendered on 15 August and Britain raced to retake control of Hong Kong and to re-establish it as a functioning colony. It was a bleak landscape that confronted the Royal Navy fleet that arrived a few days later.

A small group of administrators, including Cowperthwaite, had been assembled in London in 1943, charged with planning the resumption of British rule in Hong Kong. This Hong Kong Planning Unit was led by a charismatic leader, David MacDougall, who had escaped from Hong Kong in a torpedo boat on the day of the surrender despite being wounded (Monnery 2017). Not knowing that the war would be foreshortened by the use of atomic bombs, the unit had assumed a much slower end to the war, but they threw themselves into the recovery programme with gusto.

MacDougall was supported by Geoffrey Follows, who would be Hong Kong's first post-war financial secretary. Follows decided to aim for a rapid rehabilitation of the economy. With no reserves and no funds coming from Britain this seemed ambitious. And yet the establishment of peace and a functioning government unleashed a wave of successful entrepreneurialism.

CUBA AND THE RISE OF BATISTA

Cuba also had an eventful first half of the twentieth century. In 1906, four years after achieving independence, Cuba conduced a disputed election. Under the provisions of the Platt Agreement, the US occupied Cuba and appointed a governor to prepare for fresh elections in 1908, after which a succession of Cuban presidents ran the country with mixed results.

The United States was as intimately involved with the Cuban economy as it was with its politics. The sugar industry remained the bedrock of the Cuban economy. Sugar consumption had exploded as the world's population, urbanization and incomes rose over the 19th and 20th centuries. Between 1820 and 1925 world production increased from 0.4 million tonnes to 25 million tonnes. In the mid-1920s Cuba produced over five million tonnes of sugar, about 20% of world production (Pérez-López 1991). US companies played an increasing role not only in the ownership of sugar plantations in Cuba but also in sugar processing and distribution. These companies placed much of their processing capacity in the US and were building their sugar growing activities inside the US too. Cuban sugar production was largely focused on the lower value-added element of growing rather than processing.

Even so, this would in many ways be the relative high-point of the sugar industry, further enhanced by booming sugar prices in the 1920s. The price of sugar had fluctuated between around 10 to 20 cents per pound over the 19th century, but, with increased production, lower shipping costs and new technologies, fell steadily to around 4–6 cents per pound by the early 1900s. World War I saw sugar prices rise steeply, but the US government intervened to hold sugar prices at around 7 cents per pound. But, when the war ended, a speculative bubble drove sugar prices to over 20 cents per pound by May 1920. The frenzy of speculation became known as the 'Dance of the Millions', as property values soared on the back of the sugar price (Pérez-López 1991). Many borrowed heavily against the value of their land and plantations to participate in the bubble, and when the price collapsed later that year to below 5 cents per pound, there was a wave of bankruptcies and repossessions. With land prices low, US firms further consolidated their grip on Cuban plantations. By 1925 US interests controlled 40% of all mills and accounted for over 60% of the harvest. US tariffs following the Great Depression created strong incentives for American firms to bring production and processing onshore, and with the world price for sugar broadly flat at around 3–5 cents per pound between 1920 and 1960, the industry languished.

Over the next few decades US involvement extended to owning 50% of the railway system, the bulk of the telephone industry, most of the utilities, and a large part of the tourist infrastructure that served Americans visiting the island. Tourism received a boost when the US adopted prohibition between 1920 and 1933.

The alcohol and casino industries attracted the interest of the mafia, who would extend their activities in Cuba. A heady mix of celebrities (including writers such as Hemingway) and gangsters passed through Cuba between the 1930s and the 1950s.

Political turmoil in the 1930s was amplified by economic issues caused by the US adopting protectionist policies, which particularly affected the sugar industry. After a string of short-lived leaders and increasing political involvement by factions in the army, Fulgencio Batista emerged as the effective ruler of Cuba.

Batista was born in 1901 into a poor Cuban family, leaving school early to work. He only completed his elementary education later at night-school. He was mixed-race and he is the only non-white Cuban to have been president. His father had fought in the war of independence, and Batista joined the army as a private, aged 20. He rose to the rank of sergeant and in 1933 was a leading figure in a coup called the Sergeants' Revolt, when a group of non-commissioned officers demanded better conditions and prospects for soldiers (Gott 2004). The coup caused the downfall of the government, and a junta took control. Batista was put in charge of the army and dramatically changed the composition of the officer corp. This would provide him with his power base in the years ahead.

A succession of rebels took the office of president, before a presidential election was declared in 1936. This was won by José Miguel Gómez, but Batista engineered his impeachment later that year, and his vice president, Frederico Laredo Brú, would take over the presidency until 1940 (Domínguez 1978). In 1940 a new constitution was adopted, giving, among other things, greater access to healthcare and more rights to workers.

Batista was elected president in 1940 and served until 1944, promoting significant social reforms but also maintaining good relations with US interests. By the time of World War II, two-thirds of Cuban businesses were US owned, and 80% of Cuba's trade was with the US. Under the constitution he could not run again in 1944 and he moved to live in Florida.

Under his successor, Ramón Grau San Martín, the quality of governance eroded, but there was economic progress. In 1948 Grau's protégé, Carlos Prío Socarrás took over and the economic expansion continued, raising living standards and facilitating the growth of the middle class (Domínguez 1978). Batista decided to return and run for president in the 1952 elections. When it looked certain he would lose he launched a coup, suspended the constitution, revoked many rights and aligned himself strongly with landowners, the elite and the United States.

The 1950s saw increasing crony capitalism in Cuba. Corruption increased rapidly and it was necessary to pay off numerous parties to operate a business. The mix of an autocratic and corrupt government, with significant US involvement, and the presence of the mafia meant that the ordinary worker shared less and less in any economic progress and their lives were increasingly controlled by others. The conditions were ripe for a reaction, and that would be provided by Castro and his 26th of July Movement leading a broad coalition demanding change.

EVENLY MATCHED

By the late 1950s Hong Kong and Cuba were about to embark on very different economic and political paths. At the starting line both economies were delivering around the same income per capita, with incomes similar to that enjoyed by Zambia or Cambodia today, Britain in the 1840s or the United States in the 1870s. Whilst not rich, their living standards were well above subsistence level.

There was no obvious reason to think that Hong Kong was advantaged relative to Cuba. Cuba had a successful agricultural industry and a thriving tourist sector. With much less by way of natural resources, Hong Kong had developed as a successful trading entrepôt. Both Cuba and Hong Kong were populated with people who had developed firms and industries, and both Cuban and Chinese people would continue to show entrepreneurialism in different settings in the years ahead. In looking at their locations, people and histories there would be no easy way to predict which would be the more successful in the years ahead.

TWO MEN

Modern economics has very little to say about the role played by key individuals in determining the relative success and failure of economies. And yet Cowperthwaite and Guevara personally played a decisive part in determining their respective economic policies. Undoubtably they were constrained by the situation they were in, but they would both regularly go against the prevailing consensus. And they were both strong and persuasive proponents of their very different economic doctrines. If they had been different people, it seems likely Hong Kong would have drifted a little closer to the mixed-economy model prevalent at that time in Britain, and Cuba would have drifted towards the Soviet planning models then common in Eastern Europe.

Milton Friedman, the Nobel-winning economist, was in no doubt that Cowperthwaite was a prime factor in Hong Kong's success. He visited Hong Kong in 1955, and again in 1963, when he met Cowperthwaite, finding him hugely impressive. Later, in 1997, he gave a speech about the success of Hong Kong, noting its extraordinary growth:

From 1960 to 1996, per capita income in Hong Kong rose from about one-quarter of that in Britain to a third larger. It's easy to state those figures. It is more difficult to realize their significance. Compare Britain, the source of the industrial revolution, the economic superpower in the nineteenth century, with Hong Kong, a spit of land, overpopulated, overcrowded, no resources except for a great harbor. Yet this spit of overcrowded land is able within four decades to provide its people with a level of income one-third higher than the income enjoyed by the residents of its mother country.[18]

Friedman was certain that there was a very clear reason for the difference in the performance of Britain and Hong Kong:

> The big difference is in economic policy. Hong Kong followed a very different economic policy than [Britain].... The difference was a pure accident that the Colonial Office in Britain happened to send John Cowperthwaite, now Sir John Cowperthwaite, to Hong Kong to serve as its Financial Secretary.

Others were equally in no doubt of the impact that Guevara had on Cuban policy, and the world more generally. Jean-Paul Sartre came to Cuba in 1960 and had deep discussions with Guevara. He was full of praise for him (Sinclair 1968):

> I admire Che Guevara. In fact, I believe that the man was not only an intellectual but also the most complete human being of our age: as a fighter and as a man, as a theoretician who was able to further the cause of revolution by drawing his theories from his personal experience in battle.

And when Nelson Mandela visited Cuba he too paid homage to Guevara:

> We also honour the great Che Guevara, whose revolutionary exploits, including on our own continent, were too powerful for any prison censors to hide from us. The life of Che is an inspiration to all human beings who cherish freedom. We will always honour his memory.[19]

Even senior officials at the US Treasury begrudgingly respected Guevara:

> Guevara knows and understands foreign exchange, balance of payments etc., And in fact he understands finance and economics, and he knows exactly where the hell he is going.... It [is] just like talking to another banker, except the son of a bitch is an orthodox Marxist.[20]

THE ROLE OF THE INDIVIDUAL

It seems odd that economists place so little emphasis on individuals. But even historians cannot decide on the importance that key protagonists play in shaping how events unfold. Some believe that the development of economies and societies follows a largely predetermined direction. For Marxists, such as Guevara, the move from feudalism to capitalism to socialism and eventually to communism is inevitable. The individual can participate in this movement, but the source of the energy that drives change is that of differing class interests, not individual heroes. Whig historians (such as Macaulay 1848), also rejected the role of the heroic individual in favour of a belief that society inevitably advances towards greater enlightenment and prosperity embodied in liberal democracy, scientific progress and personal freedoms. Whilst Marxists and Whigs differed in their destinations, both believed individuals can do little to affect the outcome.

Another challenge to the role of the individual leader has come from the 'history from below' movement (Thompson 1966). Where previously it was claimed that 'the history of the world is but the biography of great men' (Carlyle 1841), others would argue that historical leaders are no more than the products of their times (Spencer 1896) or that it is the life experiences of ordinary people more broadly rather than the actions and impact of a few that is important (Morton 1938; Thompson 1963; Zinn 1980).

What is clear is that Guevara and Cowperthwaite were charged with making critical decisions about what economic policies should be adopted. Others may well have reached different conclusions. Theirs was not an unbounded choice; they were constrained by the history and circumstances of the environment in which they operated. And it may well be that in more stable and uninteresting times they would not have had the same influence. Perhaps it was because they were central actors at a crossroads in history that gave them importance (Hook 1943). Whatever the reason, few can doubt that they, as individuals, had an impact on the paths that their economies would follow.

Guevara, as an avid student of Marx, would often argue that there was an inevitability to the path of history. But he also believed in the agency of the individual. Whilst accepting the historical determinism of Marxism, he argued that (Guevara 1967):

> The revolution is not an apple that falls when it is ripe. You have to make it fall.

Cowperthwaite had no doubt that individuals played a vital role in constructing and transforming their own societies. Throughout his life he kept at hand a copy of Adam Smith's *Wealth of Nations*, with its narrative of how individual action could be to the benefit of society as a whole. The other book he kept near at hand was Edward Gibbon's *Decline and Fall of the Roman Empire*.[21] Coincidentally, both books were published in 1776 but have spoken to leaders for nearly two and a half centuries. Gibbon's work was the embodiment of Enlightenment history, drawing on facts, sources, culture and scientific advancement to document the unfolding of events and to argue about causes and outcomes. Where Adam Smith focused on why some nations were richer than others, Gibbons attempted to explain why the Roman Empire fell. For Cowperthwaite there was no inevitability about the future. It would be possible for societies to grow and prosper, but equally to decline and fall.

GROWING UP

Cowperthwaite was born in Edinburgh on 25 April 1915, and Guevara thirteen years later in Rosario, Argentina, on 14 May 1928. Both were born into solidly middle-class families. Cowperthwaite's father was a government surveyor of taxes and Guevara's father was a not particularly successful businessman. They were both the firstborn in their families, and both were named after their fathers. Cowperthwaite had a brother, who would become a senior civil servant, and a sister, who became a teacher. Guevara was the eldest of five.

Cowperthwaite was a diligent student and attended the prestigious Merchiston Castle School, a private school in Edinburgh. Guevara's early education was frequently interrupted by bouts of severe asthma. Often, he would be unable to attend school and would be taught at home by his mother, who was a thoroughly unconventional woman. Raised in a prosperous Buenos Aires family, she was educated at a convent, but this did not stop her being an early feminist willing to defy convention to drive, smoke and wear trousers (Guevara and Vincent 2017). She ran a bohemian household with many guests, but she was firm in her belief that self-discipline and study were key attributes. Guevara went to high school in Cordoba, where he dipped into a wide range of subjects including science, philosophy and literature. He was an enthusiastic if occasionally erratic student.

The young Cowperthwaite was increasingly interested in studying Latin and ancient Greek, and won a Spence Bursary to read Classics at St Andrews University between 1933 and 1937. After graduating with a first-class degree from St Andrews, he studied Classics again at Christ's College, Cambridge, between 1937 and 1939, graduating with a double first (Monnery 2017). If World War II had not intervened, one can imagine that Cowperthwaite would have ended up teaching classics at a leading private school or at a university, and there was a hint of the professor about him in later life. Instead, as the world started to slide into war, Cowperthwaite returned to St Andrews and took an accelerated degree in economics and political science, gaining first-class honours in 1940.

Guevara had planned to become an engineer but at the last moment switched to medicine. It is unclear what drove this interest. Some point to the illness and death of his much-loved grandmother. Others note that his mother also developed breast cancer at that time and had a mastectomy. And his closest friend, Alberto Granado, who was six years older than him, had graduated with a master's degree in biochemistry and had become a medical assistant before taking a post at a leper colony in San

Francisco del Chañar in 1947. Whatever the motivation, Guevara started his medical studies at the University of Buenos Aires in 1948 (Anderson 1997). He seemed more gripped by his extra-curricular activities, and planning his long motorcycle trips, than his studies. Indeed, he nearly skipped his last year to travel, but under family pressure stayed to graduate as a doctor in June 1953. Guevara chose not to practice medicine in Argentina, but instead set out on another grand journey. His next few years would see him blend travel, medicine and revolution.

Cowperthwaite and Guevara had interests beyond the academic. Despite his asthma, Guevara, like Cowperthwaite, was a keen rugby player. They both played at university, Cowperthwaite for St Andrews and Christ's College, and Guevara for Club Universitario de Buenos Aires. In the summer Cowperthwaite played cricket, and later in life also golf and bowls. Guevara enjoyed football, golf and cycling. He was an avid player of chess, a game he learnt from his father when he was around 12 years old. Both men read widely throughout their lives. Cowperthwaite tended to read 18th century French literature in its original language throughout his life. Guevara loved poetry, as well as novels by Kafka, Camus and Sartre and South American writers such as Quiroga, Alegria, Dario and Icaza.

Neither man showed particular signs of being interested in politics in their early years. Although Guevara's father was involved in anti-fascist movements in Argentina, Guevara himself was not active in political movements as a young man, even as Perón came to power (Gonzalez 2004). It would only be later that the two men would emerge, in very different ways, to take on the responsibility for economic policies that would affect millions.

In 1941 Cowperthwaite was called up to serve in the Cameronians (Scottish Rifles) during which he applied to join the Hong Kong Cadets. He was appointed as a Cadet in November 1941 and was fortunate not to have left immediately for Hong Kong (Monnery 2017). If he had, he would have spent World War II in a Japanese prisoner-of-war camp. Instead, Cowperthwaite served in Sierra Leone in the colonial secretariat and as a district officer between 1942 and early 1945. In April 1945 he joined the Hong Kong Planning Unit in London. When he arrived in Hong Kong at the beginning of November 1945, he would find a desolate, barren, broken territory, whose population had shrunk to around a third of the pre-war level, and where everything that could be moved had been plundered by the Japanese.

FORMATIVE EXPERIENCES

Cowperthwaite and Guevara were both deep and original thinkers. But neither came into adulthood with a fully formed set of views and beliefs. The strong convictions that would play such an important part in their later lives would be built on a set of formative experiences drawn from a mix of study, thought and deeds.

Two formative experiences greatly influenced Cowperthwaite. One was his study of classical economics, starting as a student of James Wilkie Nisbet in 1940, and which continued throughout his life. It gave him a model of how the world might work. The second, more focused on how the world does work, was his role in the Department of Supplies, Transport and Industry (DST&I) between 1945 and 1950 in post-war Hong Kong. Here he grappled with how Hong Kong could recover after the Japanese occupation, and what role the government should play in that. It would lead to successes and setbacks, and through this practical application of economic leadership he could learn much about how his ideas worked in practice.

Where Cowperthwaite absorbed theory and then learnt with practice, Guevara used experience to develop a more general theory. Guevara's formative experiences were his famous pan-continental motorcycle trips and his time in Guatemala. The motorcycle trips gave Guevara a broad perspective on the challenges faced by the most disadvantaged people of Latin America. It created in him a desire to address these issues, and to find a way to do that beyond medicine. He developed his ideas as to how to put this into practice when he found himself in Guatemala during the overthrow of the left-wing Árbenz government in 1954, when counter-revolutionaries reversed that change with the support of the United States.

Both Cowperthwaite's free-market economics and Guevara's Marxism developed and evolved over their lives. Experiences reinforced their beliefs, and ever deeper and wider reading strengthened their views. With layer built upon layer their core beliefs were reinforced. Both would make decisions based on an ever-deeper perspective of how the world worked.

THE ROUTE TO REVOLUTION

Guevara's first expedition was driven by a desire for adventure and a wish to know more about Argentina rather than any revolutionary zeal. In January 1950, at the start of the university summer holidays, he set off on his own on a motorized bicycle that he had built. He headed north to the mountainous, isolated vastness of the High Andes. The 4,500-kilometre journey would take nearly two months, and he first headed to San Francisco del Chañar, where his friend Granado worked in a leper colony. He was very moved by his time living in the leper colony. The lepers were outcasts from their own society and were treated very badly. Despite this they had built their own new community, which was largely self-sufficient. In their new community the lepers had value and purpose. For Guevara their courage and proactive search for dignity provoked strong feelings of empathy and compassion, which he noted in his *Motorcycle Diaries* (Guevara 1996).

The success of this first trip made Guevara impatient for further adventures, and in January 1952 he set off with Granado on his 1939 Norton 500cc motorcycle named La Poderosa. The journey would encompass Argentina, Chile, Peru, Ecuador, Columbia, Venezuela, Panama and Miami. The journey solidified Guevara's belief in the Latin American identity, symbolized by his visit to Machu Picchu. He started to consider what had eroded the wealth of that civilization, and what could bring it back. In Chile they visited the copper mines at Chuquicamata, run by US companies, and they saw the contrast between the wealth of multinationals and the poverty of the indigenous people. Guevara began to see foreign capitalists as an exploitative force, and capitalism more generally as a cause of indigenous poverty. When they visited the leper colony of San Pablo in the Peruvian Amazon rain forest, Guevara contemplated whether he should continue his training to be a conventional doctor, or should respond to what he had experienced by following a different path. He increasingly identified with the poor and the oppressed and wanted to improve their lot. He met several Marxists on the journey and would have long discussions with them about how to improve the world for the dispossessed.

With these seeds planted in his mind, Guevara returned to Buenos Aires to finish his studies as quickly as he could. After qualifying as a doctor, he set off again in July 1953, first meeting Granado at the Amazonian leper colony. From there they travelled to Bolivia, where the conservative government had just been overthrown by the Movimiento Nacionalista Revolucionario (or MNR) a year earlier. There was a heated debate there between those who wanted to push further on land reform, nationalization, extending the right to vote and increasing state spending and those who wanted to be more moderate. Guevara saw the tensions between the forces of revolution and counter-revolution, but only saw the early stages of the hyperinflation that followed as the peso fell from 60 to 12,000 to the US dollar, wiping out savings and causing an economic slump.

The pair headed for Peru, where Guevara met up with Hugo Pesce, a communist doctor who would greatly influence Guevara, and then on to Guatemala. They arrived in Guatemala City in December 1953. It would be an instrumental period of Guevara's life and many would argue that 'what is beyond doubt is that Guevara left Guatemala eight months after his arrival as a different person' (Gonzalez 2004).

The Guatemalan economy was dominated by the US-owned United Fruit Company (known locally as La Yuani). After World War II, the Guatemalan government under Rafael Arévalo started economic reforms, and in particular land reform involving the redistribution of land. In 1951 Jacobo Árbenz, who had served in Arévalo's government, was elected to continue the reforms. But the forces against the reforms had hardened. United

Fruit was well connected in Washington and reframed the issue as one of defending the Americas against communism.

The Árbenz government was overthrown by a US-financed military coup d'état led by Carlos Castillo Armas. Guevara arrived a few months before the coup occurred and had a ring-side seat as events unfolded. Although he did not get actively involved beyond registering as a doctor with the fighters, Guatemala was a formative experience in his radicalization. He hardened his hostility towards colonial and US exploitation, he became more interested in socialism and Marxism and he started idealizing the Soviet Union. Observing that a fellow anti-government refugee was of average intelligence, he argued:

> he is sufficiently capable to realize that the only road for the working class is communism.[22]

Alongside thoughts on what to do, Guevara learnt lessons in Guatemala on how to do it. He saw the organization of Armas, and his use of his small fighting force. And he saw how disorganized the defence was, and how it was poorly led. He started his journey on how to manage revolution.

But for now, he headed to Mexico City. There he would mingle with Cuban exiles, and in July 1955 he met Fidel Castro and was immediately won over by him. Although they shared a broad belief in reform, they both saw that the more immediate requirement was for action. And specifically, action by an armed cadre to overthrow the Cuban government.

THE ROUTE TO FREE MARKET ECONOMICS

At the outbreak of World War II, Cowperthwaite took an accelerated one-year degree in economics, studying under a young economist called James Wilkie Nisbet, who had recently arrived at St Andrews. It would prove to be a formative experience for the intellectual Cowperthwaite.

Nisbet (1903–1974) had served as assistant to W. R. Scott, the Adam Smith Professor of Political Economy at Glasgow. In 1935 he moved to St Andrews as a lecturer, and in only three years became a reader in political economy. He would be appointed as professor of political economy in 1947, a post he held until his retirement in 1970.

Nisbet was a classical economist, and in 1929 he wrote his first book, *A Case for Laissez-Faire*. The book is an unusual mix of classical economics, utilitarian philosophy and the new work of Freud and Jung in understanding human behaviour. It was an attempt to create an economic, philosophical and behavioural case for laissez-faire. Nisbet was seen as 'a noted intellectual figure at the university, and a resolute free trader'.

Alan Peacock, who would later become professor of economics at the University of York, studied political economy under Nesbitt in 1940–1942 and wrote that Nisbet was a wide-ranging thinker:

> The broad course in Political Economy devised by Professor Nisbet with its strong emphasis on the historical and political background to economic policy has not only offered a useful general education to generations of non-specialists but has

taught the would-be professional economist that he must take some responsibility for devising realistic policy measures.[23]

As the subject of economics became more theoretical, more mathematical and more compartmentalized, Nisbet remained firmly grounded in the classical approach. Peacock also remembered that Nisbet was a political economist in the footsteps of Adam Smith:

> When I was one of his students, the Keynesian revolution had hardly taken hold and the consequential developments in technique which required all economists to be fair mathematicians and good applied statisticians were far in the future. In parallel with these changes, Western economists, following the influence of logical positivism, have tried to remove the judgments of value from their economic analysis, and economic policy is regarded in the fashionable and incomprehensible jargon as a problem of 'maximizing society's objective function, subject to constraints'. Professor Nisbet has stoutly resisted these changes, firmly adhering to Mill's principle that to be a good economist one must be something more than a technocrat.

Under Nisbet, Cowperthwaite studied Adam Smith and his monumental work *An Inquiry into the Nature and Causes of the Wealth of Nations*. It would be Cowperthwaite's task in later life to cause an increase in the wealth of Hong Kong, and many of his ideas as to how to do that emerge from the pages of *The Wealth of Nations*. Smith is seen as the founder of modern economics, but he was as much a philosopher as an economist, and his approach to economics was a mix of moral philosophy with a rational examination of what drives the practical world. It is clear from Cowperthwaite's speeches and writings that he was enormously influenced by his study of Smith.

The classical economists gave Cowperthwaite an intellectual framework as to how to create prosperity. It emphasized: the importance of firms increasing their competitiveness through scale and specialization; the way that trade allows greater specialization and benefits to all; the importance of prices to channel economic behaviour; the role free markets have in the setting of prices; the dangers of monopolies and anti-competitive acts; and the role of government as an enabler. His work in post-war Hong Kong would demonstrate the framework in practice.

The British post-war military administration in Hong Kong quickly realized the importance of re-establishing supplies of food and basic commodities, such as fuel, and of restarting industry rapidly. In September 1945 the Department for Supplies, Transport and Industry (DST&I) was established and charged with this task. In January 1946 Cowperthwaite took over the price control section of the department, which also controlled rationing and imports and exports of scarce supplies. Cowperthwaite imposed price controls in a limited and focused way designed to

> permit margins which, while being high enough in relation to
> the normal practice of the trade to offer some inducement to
> co-operate, were low enough to afford some real relief to the
> public.[24]

There were early signs of what would become Cowperthwaite's approach more generally. He tried to understand the underlying economics of an issue, and the incentives involved, and he thought carefully about the second-order effects that any policy would create. And he was clear about his goal. It was not to get better at price control, but to get rid of it, as market forces could re-emerge as the way for prices to be set.

Figure 3. John Cowperthwaite as Financial Secretary

In his monthly reports Cowperthwaite described a typical issue. There was a ban on exporting glass and several bottle dealers had tried to get around this by exporting glass bottles to be re-cycled abroad. Exporting bottles was therefore banned. The subsequent report noted that, to circumvent this, bottle dealers were discovered to be breaking bottles because no ban existed on exporting broken bottles. The report dryly notes that 'the re-export of broken bottles has now been prohibited'. However, the following month it notes that 'bottle dealers have now adopted the expedient of exporting bottles filled with coloured water which is labelled "dye"'. The next report reveals that ex-ports of 'beer bottles filled with other than beer' had been added to the prohibited export list. By March 1947 the report noted that a new 'ingenious smuggling device has been detected': very large framed pictures were being exported with five or six sheets of glass in the frame. Glass would eventually be freed from control in June 1947, when world supplies had recovered. This skirmish between entrepreneurs and regulators would teach Cowperthwaite not only how the private sector could respond and adapt at speed, and the complexity of any government body replicating that, but also the importance of thinking about the second-order effects of any proposed regulation.

Cowperthwaite would end up leading the DST&I from June 1947, and it would teach him a great deal about the role of business and government. In order to source supplies, and to engage in government-to-government trade in vital commodities, the department had become a major trader in its own right. It had a substantial cash position since it took cash payments from businesses to source supplies when they were ordered rather than when they were delivered. This huge 'float' provided the liquidity for the government's recovery plan.

But the need to act entrepreneurially also led to the department operating outside normal government practice. Many trading staff were paid competitively at salaries well above government norms, and the accounting and auditing of the commercial activities also breached government rules. Cowperthwaite and his predecessor both ran into difficulties and criticism. He saw upfront the difference between a government department operating in a market and a private enterprise risking its own capital and making its own decisions. It was a vital lesson, from which he would generalize when he took on broader responsibilities.

THE PATH TO POWER

Cowperthwaite and Guevara could not have had more different preparations for their subsequent responsibilities. After running the DTS&I Cowperthwaite took up the role of Deputy Financial Secretary between 1952 and 1961. He spent a decade under-standing the role of Financial Secretary. He ran the economics section for a time, and the budgeting section. He deputized for the Financial Secretary when he was away of on leave. And he was put in charge of a number of initiatives, such as a committee that explored whether Hong Kong needed an industrial devel-opment bank. It would come as no surprise to those who knew him that he rejected an initiative that was being adopted by al-most every other country. He doubted that there were many profitable projects that would have been rejected by commercial banks, and in taking evidence none could be identified. Having satisfied himself that the market was working well, he rejected the chance to extend the remit of the state.

By contrast, after leaving Guatemala in September 1954, Gue-vara arrived in Mexico City, where he met Fidel Castro and started training as a guerrilla fighter. From there, on 25 Novem-ber 1956 he found himself on the 60-foot motor yacht, the *Granma*, leaving Mexico bound for Cuba. Crammed on board were 82 revolutionaries including Fidel and Raúl Castro and Guevara. After a horrendous sea-crossing, the landing at Playa Las Coloradas was a disaster, with all but twelve killed or cap-tured. The remnants fled to the mountains of Sierra Maestra in the south eastern corner of Cuba, far from the capital of Havana. Castro's forces slowly grew as they radicalized the agricultural workers.

Castro's forces succeeded by simply surviving, and over time they coordinated with other forces that wished to overthrow Batista. The Directorio Revolucionario Estudiantil, led by Echevarría, was an anti-communist student movement. The Movimiento Nacional Revolucionario, led by Bárcena, came from the professional classes. The Organización Auténtica landed a force from Mexico in 1957. Castro's forces were bolstered when the Communist Party joined them in early 1958. The coalition was united in their desire to oust Batista but had rather divergent views on what should happen after that was achieved.

Guevara proved an effective leader and he was given broader responsibilities, eventually becoming commander of one of the three columns. In April 1958 the communists led an unsuccessful general strike with Castro's reluctant support. The failure of the strike encouraged Batista to send his forces to attack Castro and the other rebels. In fact, this initiative failed, and as the Batista forces fell back in August 1958 Castro decided to switch to an offensive approach. Three columns, led by Che Guevara and Jaime Vega, advanced from the Sierra Maestra towards Santa Clara in the centre of Cuba. Batista forces destroyed Vega's column, but the other two columns reached Santa Clara and, joining with other non-Castro forces, started the march to Havana and to power.

PERSONALITY AND PREFERENCE

Cowperthwaite and Guevara came into office with an enormously rich set of experiences. Cowperthwaite had been a classicist, an economist (briefly), a soldier, a civil servant in Sierra Leone, had run the Department of Trade, Supplies and Industry that had been central to Hong Kong's post-war recovery and had played the deputy role to the Financial Secretary for a decade. Guevara had qualified as a doctor, practiced medicine (briefly), travelled extensively through South America, been a guerrilla fighter and then a military commander, and had been a deputy to Castro during the last couple of years before taking power in Cuba. Both were married, although Guevara was about to divorce and remarry. Both had a child. By 1959 the 31-year-old Guevara and the 44-year-old Cowperthwaite had packed a lot into their lives already.

Both men had travelled a distinct intellectual journey in coming to their beliefs about economic policy. They were widely read, and very thoughtful. This made them persuasive champions of their theories. It helped that the theories that they had chosen fitted their personalities and their characters. Guevara was action-orientated, sought breadth of knowledge and influence, preferred frequent interaction and was energized when with other people. He was a classic extrovert. Cowperthwaite was thought-orientated, sought depth of knowledge and influence, preferred more substantial interactions and got energy from being alone. He was a classic introvert.

Guevara was always pushing himself physically to new levels. As young men both were interested in sport, but as they aged Cowperthwaite turned to bowls, golf and (watching) horse racing. Guevara set out on guerrilla campaigns in the Congo and in Bolivia, with his asthma being so bad that he was frequently carried by others. It seems likely that the asthma that so blighted Guevara's childhood drove him to try to prove that he could overcome this disability.

Guevara and Cowperthwaite also differed in how they processed information. Cowperthwaite was more likely to trust new information that was present, tangible and concrete. He looked for details and facts and believed that data provided meaning. He distrusted (other people's) hunches. He took the same view as that attributed to William Edwards Deming, the great business quality guru, that 'In God we trust; all others [must] bring data'. Guevara preferred intuition and was more interested in future possibilities. For him, there was meaning in the underlying theory and principles manifest in the data. He had already strongly bought into the framework of Marxism, and information was processed in that context.

It is interesting that their personalities were well aligned with the tasks they faced. One way to explore that is via the Myers–Briggs framework, a personality style preference test that many people today have experienced at work or at college. We can conjecture as to how Cowperthwaite and Guevara might have been classified in such a test. Cowperthwaite was arguably an ISTJ and Guevara an ENTJ.* The Myers and Briggs Foundation summarize ISTJs as 'quietly systematic, factual, organized, logical, detailed, conscientious, analytical, responsible, pragmatic, critical, conservative, decisive, stable, concrete, efficient' and ENTJs as 'driving organizer, planner, vision-focused, decisive, initiating, conceptual, strategic, systematic, assertive, critical, logical, organized, pursues improvement and achievement'.[25]

One popular interpretation of these personality types (Keirsey 1998) typecasts ISTJs as 'Inspectors', who are guardians of institutions, intent on preserving social and family values. They are

---

* The Myers–Briggs Type Indicator has critics, but it claims to provide insight into personality preferences along four dimensions: Extraversion/Introversion, Sensing/Intuition, Thinking/Feeling and Judging/Perceiving.

reliable, honest, quiet, serious and use past experience and factual knowledge in their decision making. They test and probe people and institutions and are good decision makers. They believe that their word is their bond and are extraordinarily dependable. They manage those reporting to them unobtrusively but demand high standards. They perform their duties without fanfare and therefore their dedication to their work can be unappreciated.

ENTJs are typecast as 'field marshals': decisive, forceful and natural leaders with a knack for organizing groups to perform complex tasks because of their skill at coordinating, deciding and executing a strategy. They want to break an idea into its most fundamental parts, subject those parts to intense scrutiny and reassemble the idea before giving it their final approval. They give structure and direction to groups of people and are more directive than informative in their social exchanges. They are devoted to their jobs. They are goal and policy directed. They take a straightforward and tough-minded attitude toward tasks. They are willing to remove stumbling blocks (human or otherwise) that hinder progress. People's emotions are generally considered secondary to raw data in any decision-making process. They are impatient with ineffectiveness, inefficiency and the repetition of errors.

More difficult is the issue of character and psychological motivation. Cowperthwaite's greatest faults appear to have been a certain level of stubbornness, pickiness, pedantry (when it suited him) and a rather reserved character. His policy critics argue he should have accelerated social and welfare spending earlier and faster, but they all agree that living standards rose rapidly under his stewardship, as did government spending.

Guevara on the other hand was extreme in what he was willing to do to attain his objectives. Despite being a doctor, did not hesitate to kill to further his ends. He personally killed Batista forces, executed a traitor by shooting him in the head and signed the death warrants of dozens of those imprisoned after the revolution. He seemed to be willing to subordinate everything to achieving his vision, whatever the cost to him, his family and those around him. He had had an explosive temperament as a child and would lash out in ways that would mean that even his father was unable to control him (Anderson 1997). And he had a very close relationship with his mother that at times excluded her other children in his favour. Some psychologists argue that he had a narcissistic and psychopathic personality (Kolesky 2011). Whether that was the case or not, few can have lived as extreme a life as Guevara did.

Guevara and Cowperthwaite were completely different people and found themselves (by intent or by fate) in the right place to fulfil their purpose. They could have come from central casting. The shy, intellectual, stubborn but kind, liberal professor-turned-civil servant. And the extravert, maverick, charismatic, troubled, iconoclastic doctor-turned-guerrilla. In their different ways they were well suited to the story that lay ahead.

TWO WORLD VIEWS

There is a German word, Weltanschauung, inadequately translated as world view, which encapsulates the framework of ideas and beliefs that create the way someone observes, interprets and interacts with the world. It is a way to describe and understand the complex world. Cowperthwaite and Guevara had such fundamentally different world views that they saw reality quite differently and were attracted to very different solutions.

A world view has a number of critical elements (Apostel and Veken 1991). One is purpose: what should we do? For both Guevara and Cowperthwaite, the answer to that involved economic development, reducing unemployment and building society.

A world view requires an explanation of the world and why it is what it is. For Guevara the essential force at work was that of exploitation, whereas for Cowperthwaite it was rather Smith's hidden hand that translated the individual pursuit of one's own self-interest into progress for society as a whole. This needs to be backed up by an aetiology: an origin story as to why the world is as it is. Guevara accepted Marx's focus on the clash of class interests and added the clash between US colonialism and the struggle for indigenous self-determination. Cowperthwaite looked instead to the way that increases in the division of labour, specialization, trade and investment increased productivity, and through that prosperity.

Using that narrative of the past and present, and of purpose, a world view turns to the question of futurology: where are we heading? Guevara saw a future that brought prosperity to all and an end to exploitation, arguing:

> there is no other definition of socialism valid for us than that
> of the abolition of the exploitation of man by man.[26]

Cowperthwaite looked instead to a future where the 'freedom of competitive enterprise' continued to bring prosperity for all.

The last element of a world view is a praxeology: a methodology to attain one's goals. For Guevara this was socialism, with state ownership of the means of production and control of consumption, income and investment. For Cowperthwaite it was laissez-faire, or what would later become known as 'positive non-interventionism'.

Weltanschauungen are powerful. The same data or information can be interpreted quite differently from the different perspectives. When a sector attracted new entrants, for Guevara it was a sign of future labour exploitation and higher returns for capitalists. For Cowperthwaite it was a sign of future competition, lower prices and greater productivity. When Guevara looked at imports, he saw wealth leaving Cuba and the loss of the opportunity for domestic producers to substitute for those imports. Seeing the same data, Cowperthwaite saw specialization occurring to the benefit of all. When a factory closed or a new technology was deployed, Guevara lamented the increased unemployment. Cowperthwaite celebrated the chance for labour to move to better paid industries.

Cowperthwaite and Guevara had similar economic goals. They both wanted to improve the lot of those living in their respective economies. They both wanted to engender economic development and growth. They both wanted to avoid unemployment. They both saw economic progress as a way to improving society beyond the material. But their beliefs, experiences and personas led them to a very different diagnosis of what needed to be done to achieve those goals.

ECONOMIC GROWTH

Economic growth is a goal that has been central to economic thought since Adam Smith wrote about that very issue in *The Wealth of Nations*. The interest in economic growth continues to fascinate us, as illustrated by comments by Nobel laureate Robert Lucas,* who mused about what a government could do to grow like the most successful economies:

> Is there some action that a government... could take that would lead the... economy to grow? If so, what exactly? If not, what is it about the 'nature of [the country]' that makes it so? The consequences for human welfare involved in ques-

---

* Lucas helped integrate development economics, which was applied to poor countries, and economic growth, which applied to already rich countries.

tions like these are simply staggering: once one starts to think about them, it is hard to think about anything else.[27]

Growth captivates us because of the beneficial effect that increased prosperity has on our lives. For centuries the bulk of the world's population lived at close to subsistence levels as Malthus had predicted. A few could escape poverty either by owning the most fertile lands or via an ability to extract resources from others. But this was rare and limited. Economic growth has transformed this dismal picture, and as incomes have risen, so have living standards, nutrition, health, longevity, education and a host of other benefits.

Equally, a lack of growth causes severe problems. The 1930s are still scarred into the political psyche, and recent slowdowns in the 1970s, 1990s and after the global financial crisis underline how a lack of growth causes tensions even at historically high levels of prosperity. A slowdown in growth can create unemployment, put pressure on government spending and reduce prosperity.

Cowperthwaite believed that economic growth was one of his central objectives:

> I have always considered the fostering of economic development as one of the most important tasks, if not the most important task, of my office.[28]

And Guevara was even more specific in his articulation of this objective:

> We have only given ourselves a few goals. We have proposed for example to double the yearly income of each Cuban in ten years. Today each Cuban has an annual income of approxi-

mately 400 pesos. In ten years we intend to raise the per capita income to more than 900 pesos.* Although this sounds a modest goal, it is something that has never been done in America. To achieve this would be a fabulous triumph.[29]

Guevara wanted Cuba to catch up with American levels of prosperity. Whilst today that seems an outlandish goal, at the time of the revolution Cuba's incomes were amongst the highest in Latin America and were close to incomes in the southern states of the US. Guevara planned to out-grow the US:

We speak of 10% development without hesitation. That is the rate we forecast for Cuba in the coming years. [And] in 1980 we expect a per capita income of $3,000 - more than the United States has now. If you don't believe me that's fine. Let us develop, and then we can meet again in 20 years [and see].[30]

ENDING UNEMPLOYMENT

For Guevara, eliminating unemployment and underemployment was both central to achieving growth and a goal in its own right. He viewed unemployment as damaging for the individual, but also for society since it meant that there were human resources that were not engaged in social and economic progress. He argued:

---

* Moving from 400 to 900 pesos in ten years represents a 9% annual growth rate in incomes

Above all, the duty of our revolutionary government is firstly to take care of the unemployed; and secondly to take care of the underemployed.[31]

As with GDP, he was quick to specify exactly when this goal should be delivered, stating that the 'goal is to eradicate unemployment by the end of 1962'.

The Hong Kong administration was also very concerned to keep unemployment low, particularly in the context of large numbers of refugees choosing to settle in Hong Kong as they fled communist China. With large numbers of unskilled workers, and a minimal welfare state, it was critical that those who wanted work could find it.

PURPOSE BEYOND ECONOMICS

Guevara saw economics as more than a way to increase the material well-being of Cubans. He was driven by his experiences of the exploitation and separation of those in the leper communities, of workers in mines, of down-trodden radicals and all those exploited or marginalized. He believed that a socialist economy would be inclusive and bring meaning to human life:

A socialist economy without communist moral values does not interest me. We fight poverty, but we also fight alienation. One of the fundamental aims of Marxism is to eliminate material interest, the factor of 'individual self-interest,' and profit from man's psychological motivations

Marx was concerned with both the economic facts and their reflection in the mind, which he called a 'fact of consciousness.' If communism neglects facts of consciousness, it can serve as a method of distribution, but it will no longer express revolutionary moral values.[32]

It was not enough to just produce the saucepans and the furniture. The way that the economy delivered these goods must lead to the development and betterment of all those involved. People not profits must be at the centre of how an economy is constructed:

> We cannot arrive at communism through the simple mechanical accumulation of quantities of goods made available to the people. By doing so we would get somewhere, to be sure, to some particular form of socialism. But what Marx defined as communism, what is aspired to in general as communism, cannot be attained if man is not conscious. That is, if he does not have a new consciousness towards society.[33]

To achieve this goal Guevara believed that a 'New Man' must emerge from the debris of the capitalist system. This person would need to be 'an unselfish, self-sacrificing, frugal, fully-socialized, egalitarian human being' (Mesa-Lago 1978). People will start to see their work in a different light:

> Man will begin to see himself mirrored in his work and to realize his full stature as a human being through the object created, through the work accomplished. Work will no longer entail surrendering a part of his being in the form of labour-power sold, which no longer belongs to him, but will represent an emanation of himself reflecting his contribution to the common life, the fulfilment of his social duty.[34]

It was the state's responsibility to facilitate the evolution of the Cuban people through education, engagement, unpaid voluntary work and non-monetary incentives such as medals and free social services. For Guevara the job of the state was to provide prosperity and end alienation simultaneously:

> It is not a matter of how many kilograms of meat one has to eat, nor of how many times a year someone can go to the beach, nor how many pretty things from abroad you might be able to buy with present day wages. It is a matter of making the individual feel more complete, with much more internal richness and much more responsibility.[35]

Cowperthwaite did not believe that this utopian approach was of value for the simple reason that he did not believe it worked in practice. He used the ideas of the classical economists to predict the effects of policy, and for him the evidence reinforced his belief in the power of these ideas.

His focus on the practical was not driven by a denial that economics affected society, but rather by a belief that the role of economic policy was to optimize the public activities that led to prosperity. He acknowledged that he believed in the indirect benefits from a free-market approach:

> I myself have no doubt in the past tended to appear to many to be more concerned with the creation of wealth than with its distribution. I must confess that there is a degree of truth in this, but to the extent that it is true, it has been because of my conviction that the rapid growth of the economy, and the pressure that comes with it on demand for labour, both produces a rapid and substantial redistribution of income directly of itself and also makes it possible to assist more generously those who are not, from misfortune temporary or permanent, sharing in the general advance. The history of our last fifteen years or so demonstrates this conclusively.[36]

Cowperthwaite would often leave it to the governor of Hong Kong to enthuse about government's role in shaping society. Governor Black was passionate about developing social and welfare services, but saw a strong economy as the bedrock of progress:

> Economic progress, of course, is not an end in itself. Its raison d'être is to enhance the well-being of the whole community. Our basic aim is to raise the standard of living of our people. The best guarantee of social progress in Hong Kong is full employment in an efficient and expanding economy which not only permits but also promotes a process of levelling up rather than levelling down. We must, therefore, always carry through extension in the field of social legislation with a close eye to its effect on economic expansion.[37]

His successor, Governor Trench, had a similar view of the government's role:

> real uninterrupted progress with all our manifold plans for improving and raising the standards of living of our people. As a Government, this is and must always be our primary aim.[38]

There was no doubt that Cowperthwaite and his colleagues thought that the state could do good works, but whereas Guevara saw economic progress and the development of mass consciousness as intimately intertwined, Cowperthwaite saw the provision of welfare and services as a separate and subsequent task after the economy had been optimized.

Understanding Adam Smith's lesser known work, *The Theory of Moral Sentiments*, and its relationship to *The Wealth of Nations*, can help explain Cowperthwaite's perspective (Roberts 2014). Smith certainly believed that following one's own self-interest can bring benefits to society as a whole, as it encourages greater competition, specialization, learning and further division of labour. But in *Moral Sentiments* he warns that the pursuit of wealth can be harmful and that 'the chief part of human happiness arises from the consciousness of being beloved': not from being rich, or being famous, but rather from being loved. Or, more precisely, to be truly worthy of being loved:

> Man naturally desires, not only to be loved, but to be lovely; or to be that thing which is the natural and proper object of love. He naturally dreads, not only to be hated, but to be hateful; or to be that thing which is the natural and proper object of hatred. He desires, not only praise, but praiseworthiness; or to be that thing which, though it should be praised by nobody, is, however, the natural and proper object of praise.

For Smith and for Cowperthwaite the best way for society to prosper was via markets and self-interest in the impersonal and public sphere of the economy. But personal growth and happiness accrue to the individual in private not in public, and are built more on character than on wealth. It is for the individual standing alone and looking in the mirror to assess whether they are properly lovely; whether they have done the right thing, been virtuous and kind, generous and responsible.

Guevara, by contrast, thought that the capitalist system was morally repugnant, and he wanted the economy to embody a new morality within the system, both delivering prosperity and creating a new selfless, communitarian and socialist man. For him capitalism was a zero-sum game:

> Under capitalism man is controlled by a pitiless code of laws which is usually beyond his comprehension. The alienated human individual is tied to society in its aggregate by an invisible

umbilical cord – the law of value. It is operative in all aspects of his life, shaping its course and destiny. The laws of capitalism, blind and invisible to the majority, act upon the individual without his thinking about it. He only sees the vastness of a seemingly infinite horizon before him. [But] the amount of poverty and suffering required for the emergence of a Rockefeller, and the amount of depravity that the accumulation of a fortune of such magnitude entails, are left out of the picture. The reward is seen in the distance; the way is lonely. Further on it is a route for wolves; one can succeed only at the cost of the failure of others.[39]

Cowperthwaite believed that the laissez-faire approach provided useful tools to deliver progress. Far from being a zero-sum game he believed that all sections of society would share in that increased prosperity. He saw virtue in the improvement in living conditions, and the ability of the state to fund an ever-wider range of social services. But he saw morality as primarily an individual quest rather than one that should be undertaken collectively. And he would have dismissed Guevara's approach as a utopian delusion that was likely to fail on both dimensions. Instead of prosperity and humanity, he would fear such state involvement in the economy and in morality to instead deliver both stagnation and inhumanity.

THE ROLE OF THE STATE

Given the purpose of economic development, minimizing unemployment and creating a better society, Cowperthwaite and Guevara would differ on the methodology to get there. Nowhere is the difference starker than in their belief as to the role of the state in the changing economy. Cowperthwaite believed that firms and individuals, operating through free markets, would best allocate societies economic resources, and thereby generate good growth. The role of government was to enable this to happen. Guevara took the view that capitalism inevitably became a form of exploitation of the many by the few. Only the state could halt existing exploitation and create growth without new exploitation. For Guevara the state was the prime agent and had a direct role. For Cowperthwaite it indirectly supported others.

Guevara saw planning and socialism as co-dependent, not just to enforce the state's orders, but also in his view to deliver optimal progress:

> Planning is one of the laws of socialism; and without it, it would not exist. Without correct planning there can be no adequate guarantee that all the sectors of a country's economy will combine harmoniously for the forward strides that our epoch demands.[40]

Cowperthwaite considered such ideas irrational and had no doubt on which side of the divide he stood:

> I still believe that, in the long run, the aggregate of the decisions of individual businessmen, exercising individual judgment in a free economy, even if often mis- taken, is likely to do less harm than the centralized decisions of a Government; and certainly the harm is likely to be counteracted faster. Our economic medicine may be painful but it is fast and powerful because it can act freely.[41]

He would resist even the slightest move in the direction of planning. In reply to a suggestion that Hong Kong adopt a loose five-year plan, Cowperthwaite replied:

I must, I am afraid, begin by expressing my deep-seated dislike and distrust of anything of this sort in Hong Kong. Official opposition to overall economic planning and planning controls has been characterized in a recent editorial as 'Papa knows best'. But it is precisely because Papa does not know best that I believe that Government should not presume to tell any businessman or industrialist what he should or should not do, far less what he may or not do; and no matter how it may be dressed up that is what planning is.[42]

Cowperthwaite would be constantly encouraged by government departments in London to introduce more economic planning as the UK was doing at the time (Monnery 2017). He would normally just ignore such suggestions, assuming rightly that they would come to nothing. Occasionally a flash of irritation would emerge, for example, when one official asked him when Hong Kong would move away from its 'incoherent' reliance on the market and adopt the new norm of government planning. Cowperthwaite dryly replied:

As regards a development plan I fear it is not in our philosophy. But it is a little hard, I think, to describe our present policy as 'incoherent'.[43]

For some reason relying on planning appeared modern, scientific and rational but relying on markets appeared old-fashioned, disorganized and uncontrolled. It would require constant strength and vigilance on the part of Cowperthwaite to prevent the state from supplanting market forces, even as the evidence accumulated as to the superiority of the market system. Something very deep, very psychological, drove the constant call for greater state planning.

But Cowperthwaite did not believe in a minimal 'night-watch-man' state.* He believed the state should help the needy, and that unconstrained private ownership without free markets was not optimal. Like Adam Smith he believed that:

> people of the same trade seldom meet together, even for merriment and diversion, but the conversation ends in a conspiracy against the public, or in some contrivance to raise prices.

Only with the market mechanism did private goals align with societal goals. Where there were natural monopolies, or market failures, he believed the government should intervene. When intervention was required, his first preference was for private ownership and management with government regulations that mitigated the potential issues. He would use such an approach in water, telecoms and eventually in banking. But he also accepted that very occasionally the government may need to be a principal owner itself. A Cowperthwaite economy was therefore predominately privately owned, occasionally regulated, and with state ownership and control reserved for *in extremis* situations. His vision was the exact opposite of that of Guevara.

DEGREE OF OPENNESS

Hong Kong has had a history of being a free port, where goods could come and go freely without tariffs or restraints. For Cow-

---

* A night-watchman state upholds the rule of law and property rights, financing defence, police and a judiciary, but has limited spending beyond this. The term 'Nachtwachterstaat' was first used by Ferdinand Lassalle, a German socialist, in 1862, but the idea of a minimal state was common in classical economics, and more recently in the writings of Hayek, von Mises and Nozick.

perthwaite the open nature of the economy meant that Hong Kong firms were subject to the competitive pressure of overseas firms, forcing Hong Kong companies to find areas where they had real advantage, and could earn superior returns when up against global competition. This forced firms to increase their efficiency and to move between opportunities as the basis for advantage changed. Openness also ensured that consumer prices were constrained by competition from abroad. The threat of monopoly avarice was limited to items that were not tradeable and for which no local competition existed, such as water.

The same freedom was also true for money and investments that was also free to come and go without barriers.

> We enjoy a considerable net inflow of capital and I am sure that a condition of its coming, and staying, is that it is free to flow out again. It is also important for Hong Kong's status as a financial centre that there should be a maximum freedom of capital movement both in and out.[44]

Guevara took the view that tariffs and controls were important for two key economic reasons. The first was that he believed that certain industries should be protected from overseas competition, either because they were young industries, or because he believed that they were strategic. The second was that, in order for the planning approach to work, inflows and outflows of goods, services and funds needed to be accounted for and controlled. There was no point setting prices, output volumes and consumption levels domestically if they could all be upended by trade.

He also believed that over the medium term it was detrimental to growth to allow foreign companies to invest and to repatriate their profits:

> The export of profits by the US monopolies disrupts the balance of payments situation in nearly all the Latin American countries. Moreover, the discrepancy between investments and exports of profits is growing. This will have a negative effect on economic development in Latin America. Unemployment is bound to increase and the struggle for markets will grow sharper, especially at times of crisis. Clearly, there is only one alternative: to save their countries from disaster, the national bourgeoise must radically change their trade policies. National capital should be entrusted every opportunity to develop.[45]

Guevara was also emotionally attracted to the self-sufficiency he had witnessed in the leper colonies he had visited. And he was also quick to associate trade with exploitation. So, for both economic policy and emotional reasons he was happy to have limited integration with the global economy. He saw the resultant need to produce all sorts of goods domestically as an exciting opportunity rather than a source of inefficiency. And he did not see that removing the pressure from global competition raised prices for consumers in the short-term and removed the pressure to correctly allocate resources in the longer-term. The requirement to import some raw materials, including oil, that were not domestically available meant that Cuba could not be a completely closed economy. There was some regulated trade more generally, but a large part of international exchange would come from bartering Cuba's sugar with other socialist countries, in particular the Soviet Union and China. In return Cuba would receive Soviet and Chinese produced goods, not all of which were what would have been freely purchased (Pérez-López 1991). This further inefficiency was accompanied by the risk of dependence on the Soviet Union.

OWNERSHIP OF THE MEANS OF PRODUCTION

Given his philosophy, Cowperthwaite was very comfortable that businesses were owned and run by individuals and companies pursuing their own self-interest, subject to the discipline of the market. As long as there was competition, be it domestic or from foreign companies serving Hong Kong's open economy, then he agreed with Adam Smith's belief that the quest for personal gain would also advance the economy for all. Cowperthwaite would argue that:

> Over a wide field of our economy it is still the better course to rely on the nineteenth century's 'hidden hand' than to thrust clumsy bureaucratic fingers into its sensitive mechanism. In particular, we cannot afford to damage its mainspring, freedom of competitive enterprise.[46]

Cowperthwaite's beliefs were at odds even with the consensus that emerged post-war in the benefits of a mixed economy, let alone with the communist ideal of universal state ownership. The UK government had been busy nationalizing key industries in the post-war period. Civil aviation was nationalized in 1946. Then coal, railways and road haulage in 1947, electricity and gas in 1948 and steel in 1951. The UK government asserted that, by taking the 'commanding heights' of industry into public ownership, these industries could be managed for efficiency and for the long term. In a similar critique as levied by Guevara, they argued that, under private sector ownership, these businesses were under-invested, sub-scale and inefficient.

Atlee's Labour government also believed that by having around 20% of the economy owned by the state, the economy could be better planned and managed. Atlee was a strong believer in a planned economy, and argued that the nationalization programme was:

> an essential part of a planned economy that we are introducing into this country. They are designed to help in promoting full employment, economic prosperity and justice for all. They are vital to the efficient working of the industrial and political machine of this country. They are the embodiment of our Socialist principle of placing the welfare of the nation before that of any section and of dealing with every problem in a practical and business-like way.[47]

Cowperthwaite was very doubtful that state ownership led to greater efficiency. In fact, he was worried that government-owned businesses could use government power and resources to maintain their inefficient presence in a market:

> one trouble is... when Government gets into a business it tends to make it uneconomic for anyone else.[48]

Where Cowperthwaite and Guevara agreed was that planning required the control of both production and consumption. Cowperthwaite argued:

> An economy can be planned, I will not say how effectively, when there are unused resources and a finite, captive, domestic market, that is, when there is a possibility of control of both production and consumption, of both supply and demand.

These are not our circumstances; control of these factors lies outside our borders.[49]

Guevara went further than the mixed-economy model since he believed that his approach required taking direct state ownership of virtually all businesses and their assets. He followed Marx, who had written that 'the theory of communism can be summed up in one sentence: abolish all private property'. Cuba's collectivization would be unusually extensive, but the philosophy behind it would appear in a watered-down form, even in western economies:

> The first precondition [of planning] is control over the means of production. The sine qua non for an economic plan is that the state controls the bulk of the means of production, and better yet, if possible, all the means of production.[50]

With the economic structure set – one state-owned, planned and closed; one privately-owned, free-market and open – the question was how those structures generated economic decisions. These fell into four main categories. The first was how existing businesses were managed day-to-day, encompassing all the management decisions including pricing, production volumes, sales channels, labour utilization and the like. The second was how resources were allocated over the longer term, including investments in new businesses (encompassing any industry selection and any limits on a sector's growth) and the liquidation of businesses when they became redundant or uncompetitive. The third was the government's direct role in the economy, including services delivered or organised by the government itself, such as education and healthcare, and the associated effect on taxation. The fourth was government economic policy: fiscal policy, monetary policy and so on.

MANAGING BUSINESS AS USUAL

Cowperthwaite thought it was up to business executives and owners to run their businesses, deciding how much to produce, what prices to set, where to buy raw materials, where to sell their products and to make the myriad of decisions involved in running a corporation:

> For us a multiplicity of individual decisions by businessmen and industrialists will still, I am convinced, produce a better and wiser result than a single decision by a Government with its inevitably limited knowledge of the myriad factors involved, and its inflexibility.[51]

Guevara disagreed. As he surveyed the pre-revolutionary economy, he saw a small number of winners and a large number of losers. He believed that capitalism led to excess capacity, concentration of success in the largest enterprises, and exploitation of workers:

> With unemployment and the system of allowing economic forces to fight amongst themselves, the worker has to sell himself as a thing that works, competing against the worker next door who is also hungry. And the capitalist simply buys the cheapest merchandise: one of them is hungrier than the other, or weaker than the others, or betrays his class interests, and sells himself cheaper. This is the one who gets the job.[52]

Guevara believed that the root cause of this was 'the quantity of idle factories'. For him there was a vicious circle at the heart of capitalism due to the 'anarchy' of the laissez-faire approach. The dynamic started as new opportunities created a flood of excess investment:

> In any free enterprise system, when one man starts a screw factory and business is good, his neighbor thinks that screw factories are a great business, and starts one of his own. The result is that you have [too many] screw factories and the result is closed factories.

As investment was targeted at the sector, bigger firms used the competitive environment to overwhelm smaller firms:

> Factories that belong to small businessmen, petty Cuban capitalists [who] have to compete with great monopolistic firms, which, when they have a competitor simply lower their prices.

It required the government to nationalize the means of production and restructure each sector to remove this blight of idle factories, direct workers to the optimal tasks and stop exploitation. Instead of the 'anarchy' of the market that allowed capital to go where it wanted, and for labour to be bought and sold, Guevara believed that the government could make all the critical business decisions so that inefficiency, excess capacity and overinvestment could be eliminated.

Cowperthwaite did not believe that the government had the information, skills or incentives to correctly make such decisions. He did not believe that the capitalist approach inevitably led to inefficiency; indeed, he thought the reverse was true. Whilst government had an important supporting role, running businesses was for the owners and executives of those businesses to do:

> In any case, I largely agree with those that hold that Government should not in general interfere with the course of the economy merely on the strength of its own commercial judgment. If we cannot rely on the judgment of individual businessmen, taking their own risks, we have no future anyway.[53]

RESOURCE ALLOCATION: NEW OPPORTUNITIES

Choosing where to make new investments is absolutely critical to delivering long-run growth. Optimizing the performance of existing resources in existing industries may give a boost to productivity and prosperity, but far more important is the cumulative impact of superior resource allocation. Once again Cowperthwaite and Guevara had very different views on who should decide on and manage this vital activity. Cowperthwaite argued strongly against a government-led growth plan, instead believing that the market would sort the good investments from the bad:

> I am afraid that I do not believe that any body of men can have enough knowledge of the past, the present and the future to establish 'development priorities' – which presumably means procuring some developments as being good and prohibiting others as being bad.[54]

Cowperthwaite took the same view as the classical economists that the key to growth was that successful companies should earn a surplus profit, and that they should then use this to invest in the projects they considered the most attractive. If those investments worked, further surpluses and new investments would result. If not, then those investments would fail. His experience in Hong Kong was that this worked:

> Enterprise in Hong Kong has a good record of productive reinvestment and I have a keen realization of the importance of not withdrawing capital from the private sector of the economy, particularly when it is responsible for an important part of the public services. I am confident, however old-fashioned this may sound, that funds left in the hands of the public will come into the Exchequer with interest at the time in the future when we need them.[55]

Guevara agreed that new investment was central to economic development but did not believe it could be left to the 'anarchy' of the market.

> There is a great difference between free enterprise development and revolutionary development. In one of them wealth is concentrated in the hands of the fortunate few, the friends of the government, the best wheeler-dealers.[56]

Given Guevara's model that capitalism leads to excess capacity and thereby to exploitation, it was vital that the state did not repeat that mistake:

> When we need one screw factory, there will be one screw factory. When we need a machete factory, there will be one machete factory, not three. Let us save the nation's capital.[57]

One problem with the government controlling investment is that their investment decisions are about more than the expected return. For Guevara a perennial issue was whether to invest to increase productivity even if that meant redundancies:

> [Many] small companies were staffed by employees with primitive tools. If we were to mechanize all these industries so that a few men could do the work of many, the rest might remain unemployed.[58]

Guevara was publicly concerned with the trade-off between investment and unemployment, but never linked the other trade-off between constrained investment and the constant failure of Cuban industry to deliver productivity improvements. And with the government controlling most firms it was hard for them to proactively support investment that reduced the number of workers. Cowperthwaite could remain indifferent to the unemployment caused from new investment in any particular firm of sector in the belief that those workers would soon be employed in a new growing opportunity.

RESOURCE ALLOCATION: INDUSTRY SELECTION

Not only did Guevara want the government to control investment, he wanted them to direct it to meet 'development priorities'. Control could have been achieved through requiring a certain return on investment, but Guevara wanted the shape of industrialization to be determined by the government rather than by firms making their own decisions as to where to invest. For example, Guevara was a great believer in building 'basic' industries:

> Besides this, when we need a basic industry, although it does not make money, although it is not the best business, we will build that great basic industry because it is going to be the base for the entire road to industrialization.[59]

Cowperthwaite did not consider it the job of government to make these decisions. He was familiar with Adam Smith's exhortation to desist from this (Smith 1776, Book 4):

> Every system which endeavours, either, by extraordinary encouragements to draw towards a particular species of industry a greater share of the capital of the society than would naturally go to it, or, by extraordinary restraints, to force from a particular species of industry some share of the capital which would otherwise be employed in it, is, in reality, subversive of the society towards real wealth and greatness; and diminishes,

instead of increasing, the real value of the annual produce of its land and labour.

When encouraged to use government funds to support the growth of 'desirable' industries he expressed irritation:

> What mystifies me is how he or anyone else can determine what is a desirable type of industry such as should qualify for special assistance of this kind. In my own simple way I should have thought that a desirable industry was, almost by definition, one which could establish itself and thrive without special assistance in ordinary market conditions. Anything else suggests a degree of omniscience which I, at least, am not prepared to credit even the most expert with. I trust the commercial judgment only of those who are themselves taking the risks.[60]

He was, in any case, rather doubtful about the long-term benefits of providing protection to growing industries, arguing that 'an infant industry, if coddled, tends to remain an infant industry and never grows up or expands'.[61] Where Guevara thought it made sense to plan the shape of industrialization, Cowperthwaite thought it better to let it emerge as a result of many different views and actions.

RESOURCE ALLOCATION: CAPPING SECTORAL GROWTH

Guevara and Cowperthwaite had to address the issue that their respective economies were 'unbalanced', with one sector predominating. Cuba's sugar industry and Hong Kong's textile industry were large and critical to export revenues in the 1960s.

This reliance on one industry created a somewhat schizophrenic attitude, with industry participants arguing for support and growth and others arguing for diversification. In both cases there would be strong proponents for the government limiting the future growth of the sector. Cowperthwaite argued strongly against such an approach:

> By what standard can one possibly measure over-expansion? On what basis can one forecast it? On whose judgement can we rely? Who is to decide who is to have the good fortune to reap what I have heard called 'the spoils of economic planning'? Do we no longer put our faith in the judgement of free private enterprise? I can myself recall being told repeatedly, in the early post-war years and at intervals thereafter, that the cotton spinning industry was over-expanding. It has expanded many times since then and still thrives. I recall even more vividly a prominent and influential businessman telling me in 1956 that Government must take early steps to restrict the further growth of the garment industry because it was already too large; since then it has expanded its exports by ten times or $2,000 million a year. I, for one, will not forget that lesson.[62]

Guevara on the other hand thought that Cuba must break free of its dependence on the sugar industry. He equated 'underdevelopment' with what he described as 'colonial, semi-colonial or dependent countries' whose

> economies have been twisted by imperialism, which has abnormally developed in us those branches of industry or agriculture needed to complement its complex economy.[63]

Guevara believed that the US wanted to keep Cuba as a poor, agricultural economy serving the food producers in America.

Not only would this depress development, it also placed the greatest risk on those least able to shoulder it:

> 'Underdevelopment' or distorted development, brings dangerous specialization in raw materials, inherent in which is the threat of hunger for all our peoples. A single product whose uncertain sale depends on a single market that imposes and fixes conditions – that is the great formula for imperialist economic domination.[64]

At first the Cuban government would try to reduce the reliance on sugar by encouraging the production of other agricultural products and accelerating industrialization. As these initiatives stalled, it would reverse direction and re-emphasize sugar as its prime exported product.

RESOURCE ALLOCATION: LIQUIDATION

Perhaps the most difficult task for politicians in economic development is accepting the role of creative destruction and, in particular, the need to disinvest from low-return activities. Just as new opportunities arise, previously interesting opportunities diminish. These should be (fully or partly) liquidated and their resources reused elsewhere in the economy. But this is socially and politically hard. Even if it is agreed in the abstract that progress comes from moving resources from lower productivity uses to higher productivity opportunities, the transition is painful. The declining industry has a supportive constituency that may lose their investments and jobs. No such balancing constituency exists for the potential opportunity.

Cowperthwaite believed strongly in the market deciding which firms should survive. In reply to one legislator, he declared:

> I was particularly struck by [the] concern at the decline in the enamelware industry as an example of the effect of lost advantages, as if this decline were a loss rather than a gain to the community. It has declined, I believe, because we have learned to use our resources of enterprise, capital and labour in other more profitable directions. That is progress. We would be in a sorry way if enamelware was still our fourth biggest industry.[65]

He took the Schumpeterian* view that innovation from technology, management practices and the like provided a continuous source of opportunities to improve productivity, but that these opportunities inherently led to the demise of the old approach and the 'creative destruction' of the previous business models. Business progress and business failure were two sides of the same coin. Few politicians take the relaxed view that Cowperthwaite took to corporate failure:

> An economy with virtually no liquidations or bankruptcies is not really in a healthy state.[66]

GOVERNMENT SPENDING

Cowperthwaite and Guevara both saw a role for government spending beyond the essentials required for defence, policing,

---

* Joseph Schumpeter (1883–1950) was an Austrian and later American political economist who believed that capitalism can only be understood as a dynamic and evolutionary process.

judiciary and core administration. The four main areas of social spending are education, healthcare, housing and welfare, and both governments would be active in all elements. Their approach to building social provision was, as usual, rather different.

Guevara believed that education, healthcare and welfare should be provided exclusively by the state, with equal access for all citizens at no cost. As a communist he deplored inequality in these vital areas and would even insist that his family should have no preferential access. Rather than pay income and then taxing it, the state paid for these services and paid workers the standardized wages tax-free. This universal provision of social services consumed a large part of GDP, but Guevara, Castro and others saw investment in services as a driver of growth and as part of the transition to a fully communist society. Guevara promoted large-scale initiatives, such as the Cuban Literacy Campaign, that worked on consciousness as well as being functionally useful.

Cowperthwaite saw three possible options for social provision:

> First, public services of high standard and cost but of limited scope, leaving unfilled a substantial part of the present gap, not necessarily benefiting those in real need and benefiting many who are not in need at all (this has been our historical approach); second, public services to meet the requirements of all, with the beneficiaries making a contribution by way of fee according to their means, and with adequate provision for complete remission in suitable cases; or third, universal public services provided for rich and poor alike on terms the poorest can afford; that is, the welfare state where all benefit and the whole cost is met by the taxpayer in general. I think it is well-known that I am an advocate of the second approach.[67]

Where Guevara would celebrate the universality of social provision in Cuba as a way of generating cohesiveness, Cowperthwaite thought that universal free provision would require higher taxes, which in turn would cut growth and therefore reduce long-term prosperity and the ability to develop the very benefits that could be provided:

> What 'universalism' would certainly mean in our context is a very high rate of direct taxation and one extending much further down the income scale than at present. This is what the advocates of indiscriminate subsidy of the best may be leading us towards.

> I myself remain wholly convinced that Hong Kong's prosperity, and therefore our hopes of adequate public services, cannot survive under such a tax regime because of its economic effects and I remain firm in my convictions that those who benefit from them should pay directly, according to their means, for what they get.

> If we do not adopt the course I advocate, I believe that, sooner rather than later, we will be faced with the alternative of curtailing our plans for the expansion of public services or of introducing potentially ruinous rates of taxation – which would, in any event, tend themselves to cause just such a curtailment of public services because of their inhibiting effects on our economy.

Both Guevara and Cowperthwaite valued education but took very different views as to its provision by the state. Guevara would argue that:

> We believe culture and public health are services on which we can never spend enough for our people.[68]

By way of contrast, Cowperthwaite would rather practically argue:

> I regard education as a good thing. But we must still ask what a good thing costs, how much of it we can afford and who is going to pay for it.[69]

When he himself announced that primary education in Hong Kong would be free, rather than trumpet the success, he instead exhibited his concerns:

> I cannot say that I... am particularly happy... to extend free primary education beyond those who cannot afford to pay for it (and are already not being asked to do so at present) to the very many on whom primary school fees are no burden. There may be very good grounds for universal compulsory primary education, but I see none for universal free education, even if that education is compulsory.[70]

Guevara saw some social spending and programs to be a way to cause a jump in productivity and growth. Conversely Cowperthwaite saw such spending as a brake on growth because it required taxation and therefore reduced funds available for re-investment in the economy.

Not surprisingly, Cowperthwaite insisted that the government must balance its books, and not use debt for such spending. One reason was that he thought it wrong to pass debts on to future generations:

> I am also, I must confess, a little sceptical of the theory that we have a right, if we could, to pass on our capital burden to future generations. I remarked last year in this context that our

predecessors had not passed any significant part of their burden on to us.[71]

He was also worried that the increased demand from deficits would cause an uptick in imports, without any benefit to exports, and therefore inflation and a balance of payments problem:

> Deficit financing proper is rather the process whereby a Government spends more money that it withdraws from the economy by taxation, borrowing, running down reserves, etc.; thereby causing in most circumstances, and very acutely in ours, monetary inflation and severe pressure on the balance of payments.[72]

Cowperthwaite would suggest two golden rules for fiscal policy:

> One is that the tax structure must be kept as stable as possible to give a stable framework for industry and commerce; and second is that the growth of the public services should proceed at a steady pace whatever the speed of that growth. Given those premises, there is no necessary reason why the growth rate of revenue and of expenditure should exactly coincide every year.[73]

For Cowperthwaite, social expenditures followed the growth delivered by the market economy and had to not negatively impact commercial investment. For Guevara some social programmes were the cause of growth, and with the government controlling all investment directly he saw only the opportunity to employ underutilized assets, rather than a trade-off between such spending and investment.

SCIENCE OR SCIENTISM

There was a more fundamental difference as to how Guevara and Cowperthwaite perceived the nature of economics and whether it was a science or something rather less precise. Guevara described Marx as 'Marx, the scientist' and compared his work to that of other sciences:

> The merit of Marx is that he suddenly produces a qualitative change in the history of social thought. He interprets history, understands its dynamic, predicts its future, but in addition to predicting it (which would satisfy his scientific obligation), he expresses a revolutionary concept: the world must not only be interpreted, it must be transformed.

> When asked whether or not we are Marxists, our position is the same as that of a physicist, when asked if he is a 'Newtonian' or of a biologist when asked if he is a 'Pasteurian.'

> There are truths so evident, so much a part of the peoples' knowledge, that it is now useless to debate them. This is why we recognize the essential truths of Marxism as part of humanity's body of cultural and scientific knowledge. We accept it with the naturalness of something that requires no further argument.[74]

Guevara believed in this scientific approach both metaphysically and at the detailed level of economic planning. He believed that the government could collect and compute all the necessary economic data to allow a detailed economy-wide plan to be calculated.

Cowperthwaite had no such confidence in the ability to draw clear parallels between science and economics. For him the complexity of humans and their interactions was not something that could be modelled simply or accurately:

> I believe that [they] are innocently guilty of the twentieth century fallacy that technology can be applied to the conduct of human affairs. They cannot believe that anything can work efficiently unless it has been programmed by a computer and have lost faith in the forces of the market and the human actions and reactions that make it up. But no computer has yet been devised which will produce accurate results from a diet of opinion and emotion. We suffer a great deal today from the bogus certainties and precisions of the pseudo-sciences which include all the social sciences including economics. Technology is admirable on the factory floor but largely irrelevant to human affairs.[75]

WHAT GETS MEASURED

Guevara liked setting measurable goals for the economy, and he knew that for the state to plan the activities of each business in an economy required gathering a lot of data.

> Can you make a plan with control of the means of production alone? It cannot be done. You must have firm, precise, detailed, statistical knowledge of all economic factors.[76]

He set up a government department to collect this very detailed data throughout Cuba in all sectors. Meanwhile Cowperthwaite was being asked to collect the simplest summary data in Hong Kong, namely basic GDP statistics. He refused to do so. He argued that[77] we have virtually no economic uses for national accounts, partly because we cannot be in control of our economy and partly because our economy has a dynamism which outpaces such accounts.

For anyone confused by that pronouncement he later added:

Gross National Product figures are very inexact even in the most sophisticated countries. I think they do not have a great deal of meaning, even as a basis of comparison between economies. That other countries make use of them is not, I think, necessarily a good reason to suppose that we need them.

I suspect myself, however, that the need arises in other countries because high taxation and more or less detailed Government intervention in the economy have made it essential to be able to judge (or to hope to be able to judge) the effect of policies, and of changes in policies, on the economy.

But we are in the happy position, happier at least for the Financial Secretary, where the leverage exercised by Government on the economy is so small that it is not necessary, nor even of any particular value, to have these figures available for the formulation of policy. We might indeed be right to be apprehensive lest the availability of such figures might lead, by a reversal of cause and effect, to policies designed to have a direct effect on the economy. I would myself deplore this.

My own conclusion is that the expense and effort needed to produce even very approximate figures in our free economy outweigh the value of having them.[78]

When Milton Friedman visited Hong Kong in the early 1960s, he asked Cowperthwaite why there was such limited information on national income. Cowperthwaite explained that:

he had resisted requests from civil servants to provide such data because he was convinced that once the data was published there would be pressure to use them for government intervention in the economy.[79]

The Guardian, in its obituary for Cowperthwaite, recalled that he was once asked what was the key thing that poor countries should do to improve their growth. His reply was that 'they should abolish the office of national statistics.'[80]

Why did Cowperthwaite and Guevara come to such different views on measurement? The obvious reason is that they had very different functional needs for information and data given the different roles that their respective governments played in the economy. In constructing a detailed economy-wide plan Guevara had an insatiable appetite for data and measurement. Cowperthwaite let the market determine a price, and the dispersed participants in the economy could see it and react accordingly. Their difference also reflected their political approach. Guevara looked for opportunities to have the state run things, because he believed the market led to anarchy and inefficiency. Cowperthwaite instead thought that furnishing civil servants and politicians with reams of data could only lead to them interfering and damaging the economy.

WELTANSCHAUUNGEN AND ECONOMIC POLICY

Guevara and Cowperthwaite both had very well-developed frameworks about how people, economies and societies work. There was a harmony and a completeness about the way that they combined the elements of their Weltanschauungen: purpose, explanation, origin, futurology and methodology. Each was very well suited to their particular environment and provided exceptional examples of policymakers marrying their theories and values with practical policy making. It is rare to see such complete and holistic sets of beliefs, and it is partly their clarity that led to such persistent policy.

THE PATH FOR CUBA

In the months after Batista was successfully overthrown, it was not obvious that Cuba would turn to communism. The first post-Batista government had a majority of moderates and liberals, although real power remained with Castro, and he became Prime Minister in February 1959. There were those who wanted to ensure the revolution became socialist, in particular Guevara, but Fidel Castro himself prioritized a nationalist agenda of land reform and reducing US imperialism and control.

At first relations with the United States looked promising. Castro visited New York in April and met with an enthusiastic reception. He had productive discussions with Vice President Nixon, and in early May the US and Cuba signed an agreement to cooperate on technology and agrarian reform (Franklin 2016). But these early positive signs would soon be replaced by a vicious circle of tit for tat between Cuba and the US.

The first break would be a reaction to Cuba nationalizing US assets. With the military and initial political phases of the revolution achieved, in May 1959 Guevara was busy organizing the adoption of the Agrarian Reform Law. The new law limited land ownership to 1,000 acres or 3,300 acres for livestock or sugar production, respectively. Although Batista supporters received no compensation for the land seized from them, the remainder of landowners were offered 20-year Cuban government bonds yielding 4.5%. Very efficient farms with yields of more than 50% higher than the national average could be partially exempted. Acquired land was distributed to agricultural workers and cooperative farms by the newly formed National Institute of Agrarian Reform (INRA). INRA would in due course provide a parallel revolutionary structure well beyond the agricultural sector, absorbing normal government departments or just circumventing them.

It would be some months until the programme was pursued with vigour, and even then relatively few estates were affected. But the threat to US ownership was clear, with the five largest US sugar companies controlling around two million acres. The US corporations were also upset at the payment terms, which compensated them for the value of the land as stated in their tax returns. These values were artificially low, which had lowered the tax they paid for decades. Now those low values were not so advantageous, and the companies started to lobby Congress and President Eisenhower over the summer of 1959. The window for constructing a positive US-Cuban relationship was beginning to close.

CHE THE CIVIL SERVANT

On 12 June 1959 Guevara set off on his three-month trip to Egypt, Yugoslavia, Japan, India, Pakistan, Ceylon, Sudan, Morocco, Burma, Syria and Indonesia. He had two objectives: to establish diplomatic and trade agreements with these countries as a counterbalance to the United States; and to learn how other countries managed their economies. He was particularly struck by how some of these countries had developed heavy industries, such as shipbuilding, steel, paper mills and turbine manufacturing. He was convinced that Cuba could do the same (Yaffe 2009). And he was also taken by the science and research institutes that some countries had established as a way to control and benefit from research and development at a national level.

But in many ways the most important part of the trip was his observations regarding the how as well as the what. Guevara saw how the mechanics of planning operated in practice, and he quickly realized that the choices made about how to plan were vital to the way in which businesses and even society might then work. Many of the countries he visited used planning to manage resource allocation. Some also managed day-to day business activities through government plans. Yugoslavia was of particular interest to Guevara because it was relatively advanced and because it used a variant of the Soviet planning system. The Yugoslavian 'self-management' system delegated many operating decisions to the factories and the workers directly involved. There was room for some incentives, and business organizations could buy and sell to each other at agreed prices. The system was based on the Soviet Auto-Financing System (AFS)* and whilst Guevara was attracted to the development that it had supported, he was concerned that enterprises could compete against each other. He described the approach as 'managerial capitalism with a socialist distribution of the profits',[81] and worried that it was not a truly

---

* Also known as Economic Calculus.

socialist system. The debate about how socialist planning should work would continue for decades to come.

Figure 4. Guevara at the Ministry of Industry

After Guevara returned to Havana, Castro installed him in a string of positions that would make him central to Cuba economic direction (Yaffe 2009). On 7 October 1959 Guevara was appointed as head of the new Department of Industrialization within INRA. On 26 November 1959 Guevara was appointed as President of the National Bank of Cuba (NBC). Guevara would joke that at a long council meeting he was drifting off when he heard Castro ask if there were any good communists in the room. Guevara raised his hand immediately. A surprised Castro asked 'Che, I didn't know you were a good economist'. Guevara replied 'Oh, I thought you asked for a good communist'.

Later, in February 1961, Guevara would become Minister of Industry. Alongside being Minister of Industry and president of the national bank, Guevara joined the Council of Ministers, and would also take on a number of ad hoc and one-off roles.

The senior officials at the NBC had continued to run the bank after the revolution, but they had been slow to implement some key measures, such as the withdrawal of high-denomination notes in order to prevent capital flight. Guevara's appointment was to guarantee the NBC was aligned with government policy. As president of the NBC Guevara immediately withdrew Cuban gold reserves from the US, which was a shrewd move given later sanctions. He also extracted Cuba from US-led financial institutions such as the International Monetary Fund (IMF), the World Bank and the Inter-American Development Bank. Guevara would ensure that the NBC was ready to support the nationalist, anti-US agenda, and also that it laid the necessary groundwork for a socialist approach to state planning.

NATIONALISM AND NATIONALIZATION

The most striking element of Cuba's economic policy since the revolution is its very comprehensive state ownership of the means of production. Nationalization started with the land reforms of the Agrarian Reform Law of May 1959. Implementing this was more complicated than first realized. The 900,000 acres of land seized from Batista supporters could be redistributed, but the data and records for land use and land ownership were in a poor state (O'Connor 1968). INRA started to collect and verify land statistics through its twenty-eight Agricultural Development Zones.

Throughout 1959 the large US-owned sugar estates were largely left alone, partly because of a lack of capacity to take them into state control and partly because the government was unsure it had the funds for working capital and initial recompense. But Guevara was clear that the process would bite:

> [The revolutionaries] confront imperialism. They know that the Agrarian reform is the basis on which the new Cuba must build itself. They know that the Agrarian Reform will give land to the dispossessed, but that it will dispossess its unjust possessors; and they know that the greatest of the unjust possessors are also influential men in the State Department or in the government of the United States of America.[82]

But early 1960 saw 70,000 acres expropriated, with the threat that more would be taken after the harvest. The companies started lobbying heavily for Washington to intervene. They were well connected. One company, United Fruit, which had played a key role on overthrowing the Árbenz government in Guatemala, owned over a quarter of a million acres in Cuba. Secretary of State John Foster Dulles had been a shareholder and lawyer for the company. His brother, Allen W. Dulles, had been a board member of the company, and was now in charge of the CIA. His predecessor at the CIA, Walter Bedell Smith, had also been president of United Fruit. It was not hard to maintain that there may have been some mixed motives involved.

The initial steps towards state ownership of the non-agricultural means of production were rather modest (Yaffe 2009). The first state-owned enterprise was a small plastic factory and mechanics workshop that had run into financial difficulties in 1959. Its owner, a supporter of the Communist Party, offered control of it to the new Ministry of Industry. A tile factory with 20 workers came next when its owner fled the country, and the defunct American Steel, which had closed some years before, were next. Other businesses that had belonged to Batista supporters or emigrants followed under the Ministry for the Recovery of Misappropriated Assets. In addition, the government had moved to control prices in the telephone sector, and in August 1959 electricity prices charged by the Cuban Electric Company, a US-owned company, were reduced (Franklin 2016).

With Guevara's return to Cuba, and his taking up the key economic posts, 1960 would be eventful. Guevara was at the centre of all the economic strands: nationalizing land, nationalizing industry, defending against the expected US response and building trade links to replace those with the US.

In February 1960 the Soviet Union agreed to supply crude oil and other products and in return to purchase five million tons of sugar over the following five years. In March a French freighter carrying munitions that Belgium had sold to Cuba against the wishes of the United States blew up in Havana harbour. Castro was quick to blame counter-revolutionaries and the United States. In April 1960 Guevara established and chaired the Bank of Foreign Commerce (BANCEC). This organization was charged with managing and stockpiling imports in case the US imposed trade sanctions. In June the Soviet crude arrived, and the two US refineries (Esso and Texaco) and the UK Shell refinery refused to refine it. In response Cuba nationalized them.

In July the US cancelled all remaining purchases of sugar, and Cuba authorized the nationalization of all remaining US-owned business land and property: around two million acres for the sugar companies, and the following month all remaining US agricultural and industrial concerns. The USSR and China both agreed to purchase sugar to cover the lost sales to the US.

In the banking sector Guevara nationalized the three US banks operating in Cuba in September. By October 1960 the government passed new laws reserving all elements of banking to the state (Yaffe 2009). The creation of money, provision of credit, loans and mortgages and holding of savings and deposits were all to be exclusively state activities. All remaining financial institutions were nationalized and combined into one state bank monopoly. Guevara believed this would 'effectively guarantee that the Agrarian reform and the great aspirations to industrialize the country won't suffer from any kind of sabotage or obstacles from within the country'.[83]

In October the Urban Reform Law passed, under which all commercial land and properties and all large industrial, logistics and commercial companies were nationalized. When Eisenhower retaliated with trade sanctions, prohibiting all exports to Cuba except food and medicine, Cuba nationalized the few remaining small US companies in late October (Álvarez de Toledo 2010). In December 1960 the US fixed the sugar quota at zero, and Castro announced that the socialist economies had agreed to substitute for US purchases.

Figure 5. Havana cigar factory with revolutionary posters (1964)

Through this programme of nationalism and nationalization the bulk of the economy had moved to state ownership by 1961. Wholesale trade, foreign trade, banking and education were 100% state owned; transportation 92%; industry 85%; construction 80%; retail 52% and agriculture 37% (Mesa-Lago 1981). The remaining small non-agricultural activities would be nationalized over the next few years. The agricultural sector was more complicated. It would not be until the 1963 Second Agrarian Law that farms of between 150 and 1,000 acres were nationalized, bringing 70% of agriculture into state ownership. 155,000 smallholdings of less than 150 acres remained privately held by individuals or families, but even these were controlled in many ways, including where they could sell their output and at what price.

THE BAY OF PIGS AND THE CUBAN MISSILE CRISIS

As these economic measures unfolded, the diplomatic war continued, notably with a famous speech by Castro to the United Nations in September 1960. Throughout 1960 and 1961 there were also a number of freelance acts of terrorism, with planes taking off from US territories and dropping small bombs on Cuba, and incendiary devices being set off in Cuba, including in the dolls department of a department store. More significantly, the CIA were also active in plots to assassinate Castro, including using a box of Castro's favourite cigars contaminated with a botulism toxin so strong that just putting one cigar in your mouth would be deadly (Franklin 2016). On 3 January 1961 the US and Cuba broke off diplomatic relations (Franklin 2016).

The newly elected President Kennedy was not happy to inherit the Eisenhower plan for challenging Castro, but he was drawn into the plans for assassination and invasion:

> Our objection with Cuba is not the people's desire for a better life. Our objection is to their domination by foreign and domestic tyrannies. Cuban social and economic reform should be encouraged. Questions of economics and trade policy can always be negotiated. But communist domination in this hemisphere can never be negotiated.[84]

Kennedy denied any US involvement in plans to topple the Cuban government, a claim repeated in a presentation by the US ambassador to the United Nations, Adlai Stevenson. He would later describe his obviously false statements to the UN as the most humiliating experience of his life.

On 17 April 1961 the CIA-backed invasion force, made up of 1,400 expatriate counter-revolutionaries, landed at Girón beach on the Bay of Pigs. Despite being part of the plan, Kennedy was unwilling to direct US naval and air forces to support the invasion, and all the CIA-backed forces were killed or captured within three days. Guevara had played a significant role in preparing and training the army for exactly this scenario, and his reputation was further enhanced.

Figure 6. Guevara and Castro after defeating the US-backed forces at the Bay of Pigs

In reaction, Castro for the first time called the overthrow of Batista a 'socialist revolution' on 16 April, and on 1 May he announced that Cuba would have a socialist constitution. We do not know how much this was due to a conviction that socialism and communism were the optimal way forward, or rather due to the realpolitik need to have a protector. Either way it was excellent news for Guevara. The US would continue to attempt to overthrow or assassinate Castro, and Castro in turn would align himself more with the communist cause, stating, in December 1961,

> I am a Marxist-Leninist and I shall be a Marxist-Leninist to the end of my life.

The rupture with the United States would only worsen when Castro agreed that the Soviet Union could secretly install nuclear missiles in Cuba. Being so close, the US would have no time to launch an immediate retaliatory strike, and so it negated the idea of deterrence. When US spy planes discovered silos being built Kennedy imposed a total maritime quarantine around Cuba and pledged to intercept Soviet ships carrying the missiles to Cuba.

Figure 7. President Kennedy signs the Cuba quarantine proclamation

THE PATH FOR CUBA

The world held its breath for thirteen days in October 1962, not knowing if an all-out nuclear war would result. In the end President Khrushchev agreed to withdraw, but in return Kennedy promised that the US would not invade Cuba in the future. Although the United States would continue to support anti-Castro conspiracies for many years to come, Cuba could have some confidence that it could develop its economy free from the threat of invasion, if not from the threat of sanctions.

Whilst the crisis ended peacefully, it would, however, leave Cuban-US relationships at an all-time low.

A LARGELY CLOSED ECONOMY

The sanctions imposed by the United States limited trade to a greater or lesser extent over the decades, but Cuba would maintain a relatively closed economy as much by choice as by circumstance. Guevara believed that trade would need to be tightly controlled by the government if centralized planning was to be effective. The state would determine what should be exported, and what could be imported. Licenses were required to trade, and the National Bank of Cuba managed the use of all foreign exchange. And there would be a strong preference to barter-trade within the communist bloc rather than on world markets.

One of the motivations for being a less open economy was a desire to encourage domestic enterprises to replace imported products. This 'import substitution' strategy was intended to make Cuba more self-sufficient, and also to allow domestic production of more sophisticated (and higher value-added) products. It would, in theory, rebalance the economy away from sugar cane. Where Hong Kong would avoid tariffs and quotas entirely, and allow trade of all sorts to flow, Cuba would use them extensively to attempt to shape the economy. Today Cuba imposes an average duty of just over 10%, versus 0% for Hong Kong and 3.5% for the US.[85] Interestingly the highest levels of duties of over 20% apply to sugar, tobacco and coffee.

Figure 8. Guevara on one of his missions to Moscow

In this more managed way, Cuba did continue to trade. The main change was that trade with the United States was replaced by trade with the Soviet Union, China and the communist bloc. Over the years, US trade sanctions also softened, allowing subsidiaries of US firms located abroad to trade certain products with Cuba.

CONTROLLING GOODS AND MONEY

After the introduction of state ownership and control the government needed to decide how to allocate goods both to manage scarcity and so that state enterprises could plan the quantities of each product to make. Rather than rely on market forces, a ration system was introduced. The system still operates today, and in May 2019 quotas were reduced. Each Cuban family gets a ration booklet, or *Libreta de Abastecimiento*, introduced in 1962, which entitles each adult to purchase key basics. About one-third to a half of a family's needs are supplied via the ration system, with the rest purchased on the free market, the parallel market, the black market or by simple barter (Mesa-Lago 1978).

Over the last fifty-plus years, the monthly quota per person has typically been set at around 3 pounds of meat, 6 pounds of rice (although the ration was as low as 2.5 pounds per month in the late 1970s), 1.5 pounds of beans, 1–2 pounds of fat, 5–15 eggs, a small amount of butter, 3 pounds of condensed milk (and half a litre of fresh milk daily for children under 7), 1 pack of detergent, 1 small tube of toothpaste and 2 bars of soap. Surprisingly for an island, seafood is rarely available, because of the lack of a fishing fleet, and even more remarkable is the fact that sugar has been added to the ration list. Other additions include cigarettes (4 packs), gasoline (10 gallons), toilet paper (1 roll) and 4 cigars (Mesa-Lago 1981).

Guevara was aware of the problem caused by Cubans having savings or cash reserves that could be used to circumvent the government-directed allocation of resources. Those with access to cash could buy items on the black market, or worse, use those funds to undermine the new regime.

At the NBC Guevara completed the preparations for the issuance of new bank notes that would be introduced over a weekend in August 1961. For those days all flights were cancelled so that hoarders of currency resident abroad would be unable to return and exchange their old notes. Each family could exchange 200 pesos* immediately with any surplus being deposited in a bank account. Withdrawals from back accounts were limited to 100 pesos per month, and deposits of over 10,000 pesos received no interest, could not be withdrawn and were used to finance the national debt (Yaffe 2009). Around half of the note issue was never converted. With everyone reduced to very limited cash balances, hoarding became limited, overseas holdings were wiped out and the monetary base was more easily controlled by the government.

The nationalization of the banks gave the state control over money, loans and currency. Guevara saw capitalist banks as a problem:

> For many years now imperialism has based its economic power on money, on the bank, and has little by little taken possession of the peoples and twisted their economy, until it

---

* In September 1961 the black-market exchange rate was approximately 5 pesos = US$1. Over the following 12 months it fell to 10 pesos = US$1. Families could therefore convert around $20 immediately and $10 per month thereafter. A 1962 dollar is worth around $8 today.

has converted these peoples into a simple appendage of the greater economy of imperialism.[86]

THE CUBAN LITERACY CAMPAIGN

The revolutionary nature of the new Cuban government was illustrated by a number of unusual initiatives. Relative to other developing countries, Cuba had reasonably good levels of education and literacy before the revolution, but that still left one-fifth of adults illiterate and three-fifths semi-illiterate, particularly those living in the countryside.[87] Guevara persuaded Castro to make 1961 the 'year of education' and to launch a massive campaign to drive up literacy rates. As many as 100,000 young volunteers left their schools for several months to form 'literacy brigades' that were sent into the countryside. These older schoolchildren were joined by 30,000 adult volunteers, who managed the literacy campaign. Volunteers in most factories and workplaces set up after-hours classes.

The campaign drove up literacy rates, as around 700,000 Cubans learnt to read, leaving only around 4% of Cubans illiterate. It also created greater societal cohesion, as over a million people participated in this vast project. Urban and rural Cubans connected where before they had led separate lives; the more educated connected with the less educated. Women participated extensively in the campaign, ushering in a broader role in education. Alongside the conflict with the United States it crafted a powerful sense of Cuban identity and the egalitarian and humanist nature of the Cuban revolution.

Guevara promised more:

> A series of primary schools will be established; afterwards institutes, universities which will bring the workers along in a continuous chain, from the illiterate workers who reach minimum technical competence to highly qualified engineers, to the president of the republic.[88]

Following on from the literacy campaign, the Cuban government prioritized the funding and provision of education. All schools and educational institutions were nationalized in 1961, and are operated directly by the state. With education free to access, the cost consumes a significant part of government expenditure: about twice as much (as a percentage of GDP as its neighbours. Whilst Cuba topped the tables by a wide margin[89] in a 1998 UNESCO report testing 9-year-olds across South America, there are indicators that suggest Cuba's relative educational attainment has fallen back as funding has tightened, schools have closed and teacher shortages have emerged. The number of teachers grew rapidly after the revolution, to around a quarter of a million, but the sector has recently been plagued by a shortage of teachers, due to low wages (around 530 pesos or $21 per month) and emigration.[90]

Healthcare was also greatly expanded and made universally available from the 1960s. There was a massive expansion in the number of doctors, and in hospitals. In 1960 Cuba had approximately one doctor per 1,000 people. This has risen to around 8 doctors per 1,000 people at the time of writing. Infant mortality has dropped, and longevity has increased. Again, with healthcare provision free, the cost of the service is met from state spending.

Deploying Cuban doctors abroad has been a tool of foreign policy for many decades. Cuba sent doctors to support socialist countries such as Angola or Venezuela. But in recent years with the lack of economic growth this deployment has expanded into an attempt to earn foreign exchange. Currently around 30,000 Cuban doctors, about a third of all doctors, usually recent graduates, work in 67 countries. Doctors abroad are paid $125 per month for the first six months, and $250 monthly after that. Whilst this is ten times the amount they would have received in Cuba, it is estimated that doctors themselves receive only 10–25% of the salary paid by the overseas country. The rest goes to the Cuban government.[91]

In contrast to the investment in these areas of social welfare, housing has received much less attention. The government has done little to maintain the quality of the (theoretically state-owned) housing stock. And there has been very limited construction. The private construction sector disappeared in 1961, and in the 1960s state housing construction had also virtually disappeared. By the 1980s, housing starts (the number of new residential construction projects begun) rose to around 60,000 annually, but with a weak economy this number halved in the 1990s and fell further in the 2000s (Mesa-Lago and Pérez-López 2005). Significant emigration has helped, but with four million more people than in 1960 there is significant overcrowding and an estimated shortage of more than a million homes.

The government has effectively put a first world healthcare and educational service into a developing economy. Being free, these services have provided the least well off with access they would not otherwise have enjoyed, but may have created lower levels of investment elsewhere, and thereby a lower growth rate. This important trade-off has been a feature of Cuban policy for many decades.

THE GREAT DEBATE

There was broad agreement about much of the revolutionary approach to the economy. Economic growth should accelerate, unemployment should be eradicated, the economy should be less dependent on sugar and on the United States and inequality should be tackled directly. And there was much agreement on the building blocks to deliver those aims. The means of production should be state-owned, output and consumption should be planned by the state, new investment should be directed by the state into selected industrial sectors, incomes should be set by the government and government spending should address the social needs of the population such as education and healthcare.

But there were conflicting options as to how the state should orchestrate the planning process, which started as early as 1960 and have continued ever since. As with many controversies, the Great Debate can appear rather pedantic from a distance. But the nature of the planning process is, of course, absolutely vital to a planned economy. It replaces the market, and market prices, and the freedom of economic participants to choose how to act. It must make the trade-offs of how scarce resources are used, and it must direct the economy to greater prosperity.

In 1961 the first rather sketchy, top-down plan had been produced by the central planning board, JUCEPLAN. It revealed a lack of data, and the lack of a methodology to plan an economy, and an effort was launched to collect detailed economic and sectoral data over the next couple of years. Cuba looked to the USSR to improve the planning process and adopted a number of measures to create a tight economic plan that aimed to shift the economy into rapid industrialization. But, in the mid-1960s, the plan struggled to deliver the ambitious goals that the new government had set. What could be done?

One group, led by Carlos Rodgríguez, wanted to move even closer to the Soviet planning system. This involved allowing some market forces to act within the context of state-ownership and control. Firms would have their own accounts, could make some business decisions and retain a part of their profits to do with as they wished. Productivity was increased by setting workers output quotas, which if achieved could trigger incentives either in cash or in holidays and goods.

Guevara took a contrary view and saw the reintroduction of capitalist techniques as a retrograde step. He diagnosed the problem as a lack of engagement with the workforce. He drew on both his experiences in Cuba and his visits to Yugoslavia, Russia and China to argue that a revolutionary approach was needed to move away from 'state capitalism' to a higher form of socialism that altered both objective and subjective facts. His model was Mao's Great Leap Forward. Guevara argued that the solution lay in developing the New Man, who would act for the benefit of society rather than respond to personal incentives. What was needed was better communication, leadership and vision and moral incentives. For now, Castro came down on the side of the so-called Sino-Guevarist approach which was dominant in the late 1960s.

Guevara was intimately involved in developing the planning system that would be called the Budgetary Finance System (BFS) in contrast to the Soviet Auto-Financing System (AFS). Under the BFS all finances were done centrally, and the firms themselves held no funds (Yaffe 2009). Businesses received or dispatched goods without funds changing hands, since everything remained state owned as it was transferred; Guevara had been very struck by General Motors and its divisional structure, and he thought that activities could occur within the firm without actual cash being transferred between divisions. Productivity came from a focus on lowering production costs and from adopting new technology, even if it came from a capitalist economy. The workers and managers should identify opportunities not because of the benefit to profits but because of their commitment to socialism and society as a whole.

Under both approaches all means of production were state owned, and the distribution of money and goods was managed by the state. The Great Debate was more a debate about the objectives and philosophy of the planning process. For Guevara, education, voluntary work, open debate and collective activities would build commitment and reduce alienation. It was a philosophy that saw work as part of the socialist revolution and journey, whereas the Soviets thought that they were not at an advanced enough stage of socialism to dispense with the tools of capitalism.

When Guevara left Cuba in 1965, Rodríguez took over from him at INRA and reintroduced the orthodox Soviet planning approach for the 1970 plan. It looked as though even Castro was embarrassed by the failure of the Guevarist approach, and in 1970 announced:

> The Revolution is now entering a new phase; a much more serious, mature, profound phase.[92]

129

Rodríguez led economic planning and brought in a number of experts from the Soviet Union. The new approach kept – and further developed – central planning, and further emphasized the use of computers in developing the plan and in computer development but put more emphasis on measuring and managing labour productivity, capital allocation, capital utilization, incentives and budgetary disciplines. In 1971 Castro would further distance himself from Guevara's philosophy:

> Let us not forget one thing, and that is that spontaneity does not solve any problems. It is easier to change the structure than to change the consciousness of man.[93]

And the tools to move more towards the Soviet system seemed to be improving rapidly. Time and motion studies looked at labour productivity and identified great opportunities. Guevara's self-consciousness approach was deemed to have failed, and was replaced with labour norms, effectively output quotas, and incentive payments for over production. All that was needed was to implement this. Investments that had been largely politically driven were subject to pay-back calculations and, in some cases, more sophisticated internal rate-of-return analysis. This was designed to improve capital utilization and allocation (Yaffe 2009).

Most exciting was the possibility to use computers to manage the whole economy. Cuba had an electronic computer, an IBM RAMAC 305, that had been purchased prior to the revolution. A second electronic computer, the UK-made Elliott 803B,* was purchased in 1964 and the installation was completed a year later at the University of Havana's National Calculus Center (CNC).

---

* Around 200 803Bs were built and were priced at around £30,000 (approximately £700,000 in today's money). They weighed around one ton. A modern personal computer is around 10 million times more powerful than the 803B.

Then, in 1968 two French SEA 4000 computers were acquired. Cuba started to assemble its own mini-computers and started collaborating with the Soviet bloc on computer technologies. The planners of the 1970s were certain they could produce much better input and output plans, and provide better controls, with the new technology.

Guevara had also been very excited by the concept of cybernetics, where computers would coordinate the optimal production of goods in the economy. Oskar Lange, a Polish economist, argued that a computer would be more efficient at solving the multitude of simultaneous equations needed to optimize input–output tables for the whole economy (Lange 1972). Many socialist economies experimented with the approach in the hope that it would allow a decentralized planning system, with firms entering relevant data and relationships, linking with top-down targets to produce an ideal economy without the 'anarchy' and waste of a market-based approach.

The cybernetic utopia would not come to pass, even with vastly increased computer power. Instead, the material incentives would start to undermine the planning system. Businesses would reduce quality, or under-deliver quantities to make a profit. Managers would argue for lower budgets and then outperform them. Workers would adjust quotas and sell some output on the black market. Incentives worked in driving behaviour, but they had been poorly designed and led to actions that were not wanted. In the late 1980s Castro announced the period of the 'Rectification of Errors and Negative Tendencies':

> We are rectifying all kinds of shoddiness and mediocrities that were precisely a negation of the ideas of Che, of the revolutionary thought of Che.

The pendulum would be interrupted by the collapse of the Soviet Union in 1991, which in turn ushered in the collapse of the Cuban economy, euphemistically called the 'Special Period'. The government re-emphasized output over social objectives whilst retaining a Guevarist ethos. In the 21st century a new version of the Great Debate would arise. GDP would begin to rise after a dismal decade, and Cuba would need to decide how to divide the improvements between social spending and permitting increased personal consumption.

THE STORY OF SUGAR

There is no better sector to study in order to illustrate the effects of communist planning than the sugar industry. The Cuban economy has been dominated by sugar for over three centuries. Its story long pre-dates the revolution, but by that time the sugar industry accounted for about a quarter of GDP, and, importantly, for around 80% of exports. Sugar had brought Cuba wealth, but the reliance on this one crop had also brought economic volatility driven by variability in crop sizes and the price of sugar. At the start of the 20th century global sugar consumption grew rapidly, and rising prices fuelled a sugar boom in the 1920s. A bust followed, after which the sugar price remained volatile but at a lower level. Because the US was the main market for Cuban sugar, the economics and politics of sugar were intimately connected.

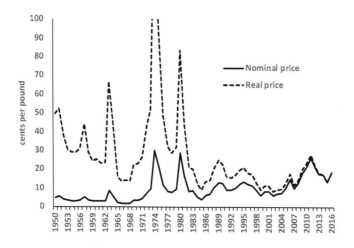

Figure 9. World sugar prices in nominal and real terms 1950–2016 (Source: IMF, Measuring Worth)

Sugar production is a fairly basic process that has been possible for centuries. Sugar cane is a simple agricultural crop, comprising giant grasses that grow in tropical, frost-free climates. There are some choices on which varieties to plant and how intensively, after which required maintenance is quite limited. Unlike many crops, it is possible to plant sugar in the same fields for several years in a row without harming yields. At harvest time the cane is cut down, using a machete or a machine. The aim is to maximize the sugar cane harvested and limit the percentage of good cane left in the field whilst not collecting debris and soil that would need to be removed later. The cut cane is then collected and transported to a sugar mill, where the juice is extracted, concentrated with heat and crystalized. This requires energy, labour and water. The output is raw sugar and some by-products that can be sold, used or thrown away.* Raw sugar can then be refined, often in the end market or at the origin sugar mill. Refining removes the molasses and produces refined white sugar. Whether in raw or refined form the sugar must be packed and transported to the end market. There are some further opportunities to add value, such as making sugar cubes, milling the sugar further into caster or icing sugar, creating syrups and tailoring sugars for food manufacturer's unique specifications.

Guevara had four main goals after the revolution: to nationalize and collectivize the industry (both the agricultural and manufacturing elements); to end Cuba's reliance on the US by selling sugar elsewhere; to reduce Cuba's reliance on sugar (specifically, to rapidly bring it down to less than 60% of exports); and to modernize the sugar industry. The first two objectives proved easier than the second two. The industry was brought into state ownership in 1959 and 1960. In parallel, the conflict with the United States closed the traditional market for sugar exports, with the Soviet bloc becoming the main purchasers of Cuban sugar. It would only be later that Cuba realized it had swapped a dependence on the US for one on the USSR, but in the early years the switch was greatly advantageous to Cuba.

To reduce dependence on sugar, the government encouraged many farms to switch from sugar to other crops. But the sugar crop collapsed precipitously. The 1950s had seen around 5 million tons of sugar produced annually. The 1963 crop collapsed to 3.6 million tons. There were a mix of causes: after nationalization farmers had little incentive to maximize production; the centrally set wage for cane-cutters was too low and so they

---

* Approximately 5% of usable sugar cane is left in the field. 100 tons of sugar cane produce around 10.5 tons of raw sugar (giving an industrial yield of 10.5%). Around 60–65% of the cost of sugar is the cost of the sugar cane.

moved to easier jobs; and the push for diversification meant fewer growers (Pérez-López 1991). Even though almost the whole crop was exported, it created a huge hole in Cuba's ability to pay for imports.

With no obvious alternative, the government made a rapid U-turn, abandoning its plans to reduce sugar dependence. In the 1963 plan, the sugar industry was designated the key engine of growth and of foreign exchange, which was vital for importing machinery and raw materials. The land diverted would revert to sugar; an ambitious industrialization plan would mechanize the harvest and modernize the sugar mills; irrigation would be improved and extended; management practices would be improved. All this would be coordinated by INRA (later MINAZ, the Ministry of Sugar) and planned by JUCEPLAN. The National Directorate of Mechanization (DINAME) would be in charge of sourcing and deploying new equipment. This would later be joined by the National Institute of Sugarcane Research (INICA), charged with optimizing cultivation, and the Cuban Institute for Research on Sugarcane Derivatives (ICIDCA) to boost by-products. A Prospective Plan for the Sugar Industry for the period 1965–1970 was agreed, which would culminate in a 10-million-ton crop in 1970 and would require heavy investment in mechanization.

However, it was not to be: 1969 saw an output of 4.5m tons; with a Herculean effort to save face, the 1970 output was 8.5m tons, but only with the appropriation of vast resources; 1971 output fell back to 5.9m tons (Pérez-López 1991). As the sugar output fell further behind plan, more and more resources were diverted from other sectors to prop up ambitious goals, causing great cost both to the sugar industry and beyond. Progress elsewhere was curtailed.

There was a myriad of reasons for the underperformance of the industry. By 1971 there were only 71,000 cane-cutters compared with 350,000 in 1958. Urban 'volunteers' did not make up for the gap due to their lack of experience. One thousand cutting machines bought from the Soviet Union in 1963–1965 were too heavy, broke down frequently and could not adapt to the irregular terrain (Mesa-Lago 1974). They were discarded in 1967. Some Massey Ferguson cutting machines were purchased from Australia, and these worked well. But, instead of importing more of them, Cuba decided to build a new machine designed by Cuban and Soviet engineers, the KTP-1. It was claimed the new KTP-1 factory would produce 600 machines annually, but in fact its opening was delayed for several years and when it eventually opened it operated well below plan.

State ownership meant many assets were used sub-optimally. Fifty thousand tractors were imported in the 1960s and were used for personal transport to drive to baseball games or the beach (Mesa-Lago 1978). It was possible to become a tractor operator with virtually no training, and so many were badly used and maintained. Castro observed that

> the former owner of a private business had a tractor and it lasted twenty years, but later, when the ownership of that asset passed to the state, a tractor lasted only two, three, or maybe four years.[94]

Castro used many other examples of a less than optimal use of assets. Light cranes broke when used with excessive loads. Electrical installations were not maintained leading to blackouts. Water pipes were not repaired and so leaks were endemic. Only 134 of the 300 train locomotives were operational. Castro would declare 1971 the 'Year of Productivity' marking a rejection of the old approach in favour of a more efficient allocation and use of capital (Mesa-Lago 1978). Sadly, the initiative only led to a small and temporary increase in asset productivity.

The misallocation and misuse of investment dulled the ability of assets to improve productivity. To make matters worse, labour productivity itself was deteriorating. There were no incentives to look for labour-saving opportunities, or to manage the work-force tightly. Where jobs disappeared, it was easier for busi-nesses to continue to retain the worker than it was to deal with the problems of letting them go. Work quotas for workers had been abolished. Even the party leadership acknowledged 'there was an excessive confidence placed on spontaneity, in the belief that without labor norms everybody would have worked will-ingly in an efficient manner…. We must develop a serious and continuous labor-norm policy'.[95] By 1968 a study revealed that between one-quarter and one-half of working hours were wasted (Mesa-Lago 1978).

One of the reasons behind the decline in productivity was an ambivalence towards financial information, making financial control difficult. Castro had denounced taking a financial per-spective, arguing:

> if we want a people to get rid of the peso sign in the mind and the heart, then we must also have men who free their thought of the peso sign.[96]

This 'excursion into economic and financial know-nothingism' (Hagelberg and Alvarez 2006) was discarded in the mid-1970s, with Castro celebrating 'the partial recovery of the economic controls and the emphasizing of cost accounting and cost reduc-tion'. The new economic and planning system (Sistema de Dirección y Plannificatión de la Economía) would 'determine to the last detail how much we spend on everything we produce' (Castro 1978). The move to greater transparency was not universally welcomed by those who held bureaucratic power. The Ministry of Sugar (MINAZ) held a conference in 1976 with the slogan 'The protection of state secrets is our contribution to the economy'.

However, the mid-1970s saw the Cuban government attempt to make improvements in investment, asset utilization, technology and labour productivity. Output stabilized and communist allies purchased the output for cash or barter. World prices were high, and so the industry's revenues rose. But, interestingly, yields remained flat, indicating that improvements were used not to raise profits, but to cover costs.

Between the mid-1970s and the fall of the Soviet bloc, Cuba enjoyed a remarkably attractive deal with the USSR, which had agreed to pay an above-market price; this continued for over a decade. The Soviet bloc paid a sizeable premium on the world sugar price. Economists have calculated that, between 1976 and 1989, the premium paid to Cuba above world prices averaged about $2.5 billion annually.* To put that in perspective, this subsidy was equivalent on average to 12% of GDP, and in the mid to late 1980s it averaged over 15% of GDP. Whereas Cuban GDP per capita rose at 1.7% per annum between 1960 and 1990 including this subsidy, the real number falls to 1.1% per annum without it.

---

* Prior to the early 1970s the USSR had given Cuba military aid worth approximately $1.5 billion annually. In addition, the USSR provided Cuba with loans, with repayments (regularly deferred) and with technical advice.

The Soviet subsidy creates another very interesting natural mini experiment. A major criticism of state-planned economies is that they mandate prices that are not market based, and lead to sub-optimal behaviour.[97] The sugar price as set by the USSR for Cuba was definitely far from the world price, especially between 1976 and 1989. But, in terms of information, the price was giving a very clear and unambiguous signal: produce more sugar. Sugar production did rise, but only because more land was diverted from other crops towards sugar cane. Yields and productivity fell. The problem was not an informational issue, but more one of incentives, capabilities and responsiveness.

With the fall of the Soviet empire, Cuba was forced to sell its sugar in the world market at the world price. The Cuban sugar industry had used the period of the Soviet subsidy to become inefficient and uncompetitive and the adjustment to market prices was traumatic. Sugar cane production fell from over 70m tons to less than 20m tons. Whilst Cuba had been absorbing the benefits of the Soviet subsidy, other competitors had emerged with advantaged costs.

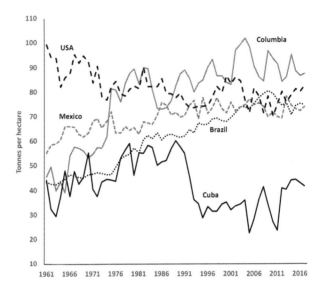

Figure 10. Sugar cane yields by country 1961–2016 (Source: UN Food and Agriculture Organization)

Cuba had once been the leader in sugar cane production, but its industry shrank from an output of 56m tonnes in 1961 to 16 million tonnes in 2016. Over the same period Brazil increased output from 59m tonnes to 758m tonnes, giving it an output 50 times larger than Cuba. Mexico, India, Columbia and others. Even the US increased its output of sugar cane. Even more disturbingly, the US was increasing its yields whilst Cuba's yields collapsed. With a lack of foreign exchange Cuba was unable to purchase machinery to use in the sugar plantations and the mills. Cuba fast became uncompetitive and insignificant in the global sugar industry.

Figure 11. Cuban sugar cane production 1961–2016 (Source: UN Food and Agriculture Organization)

Cuba was unable to organize and invest to see if a smaller, more efficient sugar industry was viable. But even if sugar was destined to be uncompetitive, the state was very slow to adapt to the new reality, causing massive human and economic distress in the 'Special Period'. It would only be in 2002 that any serious and realistic attempt was made to adjust.

INEFFICIENT INVESTMENT

The attempts to grow other industries ran into similar problems to those in the sugar industry. Guevara had worked within INRA to produce a plan for the years after the revolution up to 1965. He set ambitious goals:

> In the industrial field, the plan calls for the transformation of Cuba into the most highly industrialized country of Latin America.[98]

Guevara and the departments responsible for sectors and planning did indeed come up with a plan that would transform the Cuban economy, at least on paper. Guevara outlined how the huge push for industrialization would be achieved sector by sector. It was a long list of initiatives designed to raise output, substitute for imports, create employment and create industries that would earn foreign exchange to pay for imports. The planners had worked tirelessly to produce the plan, incorporating all the linkages in the economy, for example, the required level of raw materials.

The state had planned growth in over 200 industries, and Guevara highlighted some of the most important initiatives:

> The installation of 205 industries, of which the twenty-two more important ones are the following: a new plant for refining nickel ore, which will raise the total to 70,000 tons; a petroleum refinery for two million tons of crude petroleum; the first steel mill, with a capacity of 700,000 tons of steel, which in this four-year period will reach 500,000 tons; the expansion of our plants to produce seamed steel tubes, amounting to 25,000 metric tons; tractors, 5,000 units per year; motorcycles, 10,000 units per year; three cement plants and expansion of the existing ones for a total of 1.5 million metric tons, which will raise our production to 2.5 million per year; metal containers, 291 million units; expansion of our glass plants by 23,700 metric tons per year; one million square meters of flat glass; a new plant for making bagasse fibreboard, 10,000 cubic meters; a bagasse cellulose plant, 60,000 cubic meters, in addition to a wood cellulose plant, 40,000 metric tons per year; an ammonium nitrate plant, 60,000 metric tons; a plant for

simple superphosphates, for 70,000 tons, and 81,000 metric tons of triple superphosphate; 132,000 metric tons of nitric acid; 85,000 metric tons of ammonia; eight new textile plants and expansion of existing ones with 451,000 spindles; a kenaf bag plant for sixteen million bags; and so on to others of lesser importance.[99]

As early as 1964 Guevara realized that the investment in industrialization was not performing well, identifying a number of errors:

Fundamentally these were caused by a lack of precise understanding of the technological and economic elements necessary in the new industries installed during those years. We acquired a great number of factories with the dual purpose of substituting imports and providing employment. Later we found out that in many of these plants the technical efficiency was insufficient when measured by international standards.[100]

Whilst in Cuba's command economy the state could invest in a plant and force production and consumption of its products, it found it much more difficult to create a profitable investment. Huge sums were wasted in these efforts, depressing consumption and reducing the flexibility of the economy. This pattern would be repeated in the years ahead. Perhaps the most successful diversification that has been made in Cuba has been the growth of the self-employed sector, the *cuentapropistas*, which grew after the collapse of sugar revenues in the 1990s. That diversification required little investment and little state planning.

THE SPECIAL PERIOD

Few in Cuba realized that Gorbachev's election to the post of General Secretary of the Politburo in 1985 would lead to the disintegration of the USSR and a profound economic depression in Cuba. Gorbachev promoted reforms via 'Glasnost', sanctioning greater freedom of speech and of the press, and 'Perestroika', which aimed to reform the Soviet Communist Party. Combined with economic liberalization and the promotion of private ownership these reforms became uncontrollable, and the Soviet Union and the Warsaw Pact unravelled. First communist governments in Poland, Hungary, Czechoslovakia, East Germany and others fell. Then the Soviet Union itself splintered. In December 1991 the Soviet Union was dissolved.

The impact on Cuba was severe. The Soviet Union had been the main destination for Cuban exports and had also been paying an inflated price for its sugar. Suddenly, Cuba needed to sell its crop into a world market of lower, and falling, sugar prices. Its economy shrank by around a quarter. By way of comparison the Great Depression saw a 15% fall in the US economy between 1929 and 1932, with unemployment reaching 25%. In the more recent government-debt crisis in Greece GDP fell by around a quarter, with unemployment rising to around 25%. About half of the fall in Cuban GDP, from around $29 billion in 1990 to $22 billion three years later, was due to the disappearance of the soviet sugar subsidy, and half was due to the knock-on effects.

THE CUENTAPROPISTAS

With illness besetting his brother, Raúl Castro became acting president in 2006. Gradually, he introduced some modest reforms, starting with allowing Cubans to buy DVD players and microwaves in 2008. Vacant land was leased to private farmers and cooperative farms. Some limited salary flexibility was permitted. In December 2010, Raúl Castro observed:

Either we change or we sink.

In 2011, people were permitted to be self-employed in 123 defined categories of jobs, such as taxi driver, manicurist or repair worker. Also included were opportunities to start small businesses: restaurants, booksellers, computer services or cafés. The most popular category allowed the rental of private rooms, *casa particulares*, to visitors. Without a licence, self-employment was still illegal, and so job creation was limited to these narrow and established categories. Castro's reasoning was not a conversion to capitalism. Rather the collapse of the Soviet bloc left Cuba with idle capacity and workers in state industries, and after a decade of stagnation Castro laid off around half a million state employees. Whilst some were absorbed into other state jobs, the government needed a way to absorb those losing their jobs.

This limited market reform of allowing people to provide a service, albeit in a narrow range of jobs, has been an enormous success. Nearly 600,000 Cubans have become *cuentapropistas* (self-employed). A taxi driver can easily earn ten times the average state monthly wage of 850 pesos ($33); 2,000 restaurants have opened since 2011; 22,000 *casa particulares* are available at the time of writing, many at a price of US $35–40 per night. A nurse who earns around $40 per month, or a doctor earning around $70 per month, can massively increase their standard of living if they can rent out a room for a few nights each month.

In the late 2010s, the government tried to restrain the *cuentapropistas* by creating a new set of regulations and financial and tax changes.[101] One economist called it 'the revenge of the bureaucrats',[102] and there was a strong pushback from the growing number of self-employed. The government introduced new regulations, such as the distance between towel hooks in childcare centres. Fortunately, the government proposal that any individual could only hold one work licence, which would have made café-bookshops, restaurants with a bar, or many service businesses combinations illegal, was dropped (for now). But it did introduce a requirement to deposit 65% of any income in a designated bank account. And anyone employing more than 20 people faces crippling taxes: the 21st employee must be paid six times the average wage. And many businesses had higher tax rates imposed.

THE FUTURE

The rise of the *cuentapropistas* and the flows of family investment from the US to Cuba triggered an uptick in GDP. Under President Obama the political division between the United States and Cuba began to thaw. Raúl Castro shook hands with Obama in 2013 and in 2014 they separately announced plans to normalize relations. In 2016 Obama visited Cuba, the first sitting president to do so since Calvin Coolidge in 1928. For now, however, President Trump has put a stop on further normalization, whilst remaining open to dialogue. However, it seems likely that over the decades ahead there will be further softening of the conflict between the two nations.

There is a possibility that after 60 years of stagnation Cuba may begin to prosper. There would be a path forward to expand the self-employed sector, increase inward investment, grow tourism and the like. Cuba still has many natural resources, and the success of the self-employed sector shows there is a good reservoir of entrepreneurialism to build on. Progress could retain a large measure of the social elements that have been important to many. An opportunity to adapt appears to be available. But will there be a consensus to make the changes that such a path would require?

HONG KONG'S PATH

The story that unfolded in Cuba was one of direct state involvement in the economy, with the government becoming enmeshed in detailed issues in businesses and in the economic lives of ordinary people. The story in Hong Kong was markedly different, being a policy of facilitation. Government set the rules and took some limited responsibility for the provision of vital services such as policing, the judicial system, defence, the regulation of monopolies and targeted social programmes. But the decisions that catapulted Hong Kong forward were not those made in government offices. Instead, they were made in millions of factories, homes and offices by private people and companies. Their dispersed decisions would drive millions of actions, from which would emerge the shape and direction of the Hong Kong economy.

CHAPTER SIX

AN ANACHRONISM

It is hard to understand why a cadre of British civil servants should have cared so much about, and worked so hard for, a small colony on the other side of the world. Guevara was, of course, also a foreigner willing to die for Cuba, but he was driven by ideology. Cowperthwaite and his colleagues were not trying to plant an ideological flag in Hong Kong; rather, they were pro-fessional pragmatists. It is the same as those who work for the World Bank, or the IMF, professionally helping countries other than their own. There are foreigners who run central banks for the benefit of countries in which they were not born, such as Mark Carney at the Bank of England. There are many coaches who train sports teams that then beat their native country, such as Eddie Jones, the Australian coach of the England rugby team. Many professional experts in many fields work for countries other their own country. Why did the British-run Hong Kong administration come to exemplify this professional, pragmatic model, where their loyalty was more aligned with Hong Kong's success than the interests of their home country?

In 1956 Britain and France invaded Egypt, after President Nas-ser had nationalized the Suez Canal. The effort quickly failed, as the United States forced an early withdrawal. After much soul-searching Britain abandoned any ambition to play a colonial role 'east of Suez', and plans were made to give independence to col-onies such as Singapore and Malaya. But it was extremely unclear what to do about Hong Kong. The bulk of the territory needed to be returned to China in 1997 under the various Sino-British treaties. Britain could not return the colony to communist China before then, as this went against the will of the Hong Kong peo-ple. Nor could it offer independence, which in practice would lead to a Chinese invasion. All Britain could do was to be a good custodian for the following 40 years.

For the Hong Kong government there was little to be done about the consequences of having China as a neighbour and as a future owner of the territory. Britain was fully aware that the colony was indefensible against a Chinese invasion, although in the late 1950s the US had provided a secret defence guarantee. During Mao's cultural revolution in the 1960s, violence and protests spread into Hong Kong; however, these were contained. Most people were content to retain independence from China, but again it was a pressure on the government to deliver for the broader population.

In the 1970s China became less hostile, and not just because of the 1997 handover getting closer. In 1972 Nixon visited Beijing, ending 25 years of diplomatic isolation. They agreed to park the issue of Taiwan's independence from the mainland. The rapprochement accelerated after Mao died following years of illness, when Deng Xiaoping emerged as the new leader. His 'socialism with Chinese characteristics' introduced free enterprise reforms, starting in Guangdong, near Hong Kong, created a helpful relationship between Hong Kong and China, at least economically.

Relationships improved further when in 1979 the US recognized communist China at the United Nations. But there was a big setback with the Tiananmen Square protests and the subsequent massacre in 1989, which was widely condemned. Various freedoms in China were curtailed, and the Communist Party further tightened its grip on political power. But economic liberalization continued, trade flows with other countries grew further. And attempts to increase democracy in Hong Kong ahead of the handover largely failed. In 1997 Hong Kong reverted to China in the form of a Special Administrative Region. The Hong Kong Chief Executive is now appointed by the State Council, itself chaired by the Premier of China. The Legislative Council comes from local constituencies and sector or interest group represent-atives, chosen in a variety of ways. For the ministers and civil servants, the desire to maintain Hong Kong's success remains key.

KEEPING TRADE FLOWING

Hong Kong had a long history of being a free port without meaningful tariffs, quotas or restrictions on imports or exports. But Hong Kong was not completely in charge of its own destiny. The immediate post-war recovery had been driven by Hong Kong re-establishing the entrepôt trade for China. But, when the US had imposed a trade embargo on China during the Korean War, Hong Kong's trade with China collapsed. Disaster was averted thanks to the growth of the nascent industrial sector, in particular textiles. In 1947 972 factories in Hong Kong em-ployed 51,000 people. By 1970, 17,000 factories would employ 600,000 workers (Endacott 1964a).

From the perspective of the US and UK governments, the switch to textiles had been altogether too successful. The herit-age textile sectors in those two countries had come under enor-mous pressure from the success of Hong Kong's exports, lead-ing to the Lancashire Agreement with the UK to voluntarily limit exports. And in the US John Kennedy would promise support for the textile sector during his presidential campaign. When Cowperthwaite became Financial Secretary in 1961 the US and the UK governments were both trying to limit textile imports materially. Throughout 1961 Cowperthwaite negotiated with the UK, the US and through GATT.* By the end of the year an agreement was made for some limitations on some textile exports. But the issue reappeared in 1962, and Cowperthwaite had to negotiate at the International Textile Conference in Geneva in 1962.

The demand for protectionism would reoccur constantly as Hong Kong's industrial success continued. It would affect most product areas at one time or another. For example, in the mid-1960s the British Radio Equipment Manufacturers Association complained that Hong Kong was dumping radio sets in the UK market when Hong Kong exports rose from 2,400 sets in 1960 to 1.1 million sets in 1964. Again, all sorts of strange explanations were proposed about how Hong Kong could have the prices that it did. Eventually, after work by Cowperthwaite's department, the British Board of Trade accepted that there was no unfair competition, just better competitiveness on costs and on the business operating model.

---

* The General Agreement on Tariffs and Trade was a multilateral agreement, first enacted in 1947, which reduced tariffs and trade barriers between signatories. Major progress was made during the Geneva Round (1955–1956), the Kennedy Round (1962–1867) and later the Tokyo Round (1973–1979). The Uruguay Round (1986–1994) replaced GATT with the World Trade Organisation (WTO) on 1 January 1995, which incorporated previous GATT agreements.

Figure 12. Cowperthwaite visiting Brussels

Another threat to trade came when the UK applied to join the European Economic Community. The EEC wanted to constrain Hong Kong's ability to sell duty-free into Europe. If the UK joined, Hong Kong could export duty-free to the UK, and could then the UK export those goods to Europe. The first attempt to join the EEC was in 1961, and Cowperthwaite again travelled back and forth to London and Brussels to try to negotiate favourable terms for Hong Kong's access.

Cowperthwaite could give a sigh of relief when de Gaulle vetoed British entry in 1962, arguing:

> Britain is insular, maritime, bound up by its trade, its markets, its food supplies, with the most varied and often the most distant countries. Her activity is essentially industrial and commercial, not agricultural. She has, in all her work, very special, very original habits and traditions. How can Britain, in the way that she lives, produces, trades, be incorporated in the Common Market as it has been conceived and as it functions.

But Hong Kong's respite was short-lived. The UK applied again in 1967, and the request was again vetoed. Eventually, the UK would join in 1973.

The challenge of maintaining market access for Hong Kong's exports has continued throughout the last 60 years. It has been somewhat easier in some service sectors, but remains a key part of the government's role in government-to-government talks. But the government will not subsidize or compensate businesses if they have trade issues. Ever since the US embargo of China in 1950, it has been for companies to adapt to barriers, not for governments to mitigate. All financial secretaries have also been opposed to retaliatory tariffs. If at the end of the day a country imposes tariffs on Hong Kong exports, Hong Kong almost invariably does nothing by way of retaliatory response. There is a strong belief that it would be fairly pointless, and that it would simply lower the standard of living of those in Hong Kong.

A BELIEF IN FREE MARKETS

Shortly after Cowperthwaite had first arrived in Hong Kong, in 1945, he was put in charge of price control. With goods scarce there was a risk of profiteering by those who had obtained supplies. He soon realized the problems with attempting to set prices low enough to meet consumer needs but high enough to encourage supply, and in a dynamic environment. He quickly developed a *modus operandi* that involved encouraging the emergence of competitive markets. There were some products that could not be made available through markets, such as Japanese textile machinery, which needed to be purchased through the US administration occupying Japan. And there were some products where the supply base had not yet recovered. But Cowperthwaite had learnt a valuable lesson about leaving decisions to markets that would live with him for the rest of his life.

Often someone would call for government involvement in providing a good or service. For example, Cowperthwaite was lobbied to provide subsidized land for car parking. Cowperthwaite saw no reason why the well-off car owners should not pay the full cost of parking and why developers would not create supply if there was demand at its proper economic cost. His was an unpopular position amongst the small section of society that had cars, but Cowperthwaite saw it as nothing other than a brazen attempt to feed at the trough of government subsidies.

Even on major infrastructure projects, which, in many developed economies, are financed and operated by the state, Hong Kong has tried to use private enterprise and some form of competition. For example, since the early 1900s there had been considerable demand to build a tunnel linking Hong Kong Island and Kowloon. Cowperthwaite intervened in the 1950s to argue against using public expenditure to provide a service that would only be used by some residents. A decade or so later he concluded a deal with private developers whereby they would finance and build a toll tunnel, paying the government an annual franchise fee. Tolls were set so as to leave competition with the ferry companies. It was agreed that after 30 years the tunnel would be given, at no cost, to the government. And so, in 1999 Hong Kong received a tunnel at no cost to taxpayers, all thanks to Cowperthwaite's stubbornness in not taking the easier path of state funding.

LIGHT REGULATION

This belief in free markets has been accompanied by a *laissez-faire* approach to most industries. Generally, it is the market, and corporate success and failure, that provides the regulation.

The government has always been clear that light regulation can only be acceptable in competitive sectors. If there is a monopoly, then regulation is required. The water industry is a good example; the scarcity of local water has meant that huge investments have needed to be made in creating adequate water supplies. The requirement for water, and the concentrated supply base, creates a natural monopoly. The same was true in the land-line telephone industry, which required building exchanges and cabling whole areas. In cases such as these, Hong Kong combines private ownership of the operators with regulation, especially on prices that can be charged.

In the context of domestic and international exposure to competition, light regulation has worked well. It has worked less well in the banking sector, which has had a number of crises over the years. Not all of these originated in Hong Kong (for example, the 1973–1974 OPEC crisis, Black Monday in 1987, the Tiananmen Square Massacre in 1989, the 1997–1998 Asian financial crisis and the 2007 global financial crisis). But these cases did reveal a lack of reserves, and some weak business models.

Some banking crises were driven directly by poor regulation in Hong Kong, and in particular a lack of understanding about how leveraged financial institutions can create contagion in the non-financial economy. In 1961 Liu Chong Hing Bank collapsed due to over-exposure to the real estate sector. Cowperthwaite was surprised at the second-order effects on other banks and firms, and was very much on the back foot. It took him until 1964 to tighten up banking regulation, and as soon as he did, in 1965 a much worse banking crisis occurred (Schenk 2001).

Some argue that the 1965 banking crisis was comparable to the 1866 crisis, when half of the colony's banks folded. The disaster rolled through 1965, starting with the failure of Ming Tak Bank in January. Rumours circulated about its weakness, and depositors queued to withdraw their money. The same problem then happened in a string of banks throughout the year. Cowperthwaite found it hard to get ahead of the unfolding crisis. He did not fully understand the risk of leverage, he did not understand the perverse incentives whereby a banker losing other people's money was not the same as a corporation losing theirs, he fretted over the moral hazard of rescuing banks and he was slow to see how the issue in banking could spread to other sectors through an inability to repay deposits or to roll-over loan arrangements (Goodstadt 2005).

It would take longer to create an appropriate regulatory framework in banking and financial services. But in the end Hong Kong would make huge advances and become one of the leading financial centres in the world. The small service sector that supported the entrepôt trade has grown into leading positions in banking, insurance, stock trading, precious metal trading, wealth management and dozens of other financial sectors. Financial services now make up just under a fifth of the economy, only slightly less than the manufacturing sector.

Figure 13. Cowperthwaite arrives at Kai Talk airport from London (1968)

INVESTMENT BY FREE ENTERPRISE

Arguably, the most important policy element that differentiates Hong Kong is the way in which businesses and entrepreneurs have managed their investments in a changing world. The low taxation policies have left individuals and companies with resources to invest, with the government playing virtually no role in trying to direct those investment flows. Indeed, it doesn't even try and retain those funds in Hong Kong.

The dynamism with which Hong Kong business has responded to changing opportunities by investing, managing and then divesting is impressive. In the 1940s most investment went to support opportunities around the entrepôt trade with China. As that faltered, investments were liquidated, and a new textile industry was created. The textile industry produced yarns and fabrics in the 1950s and then moved into cloth, dyeing and finishing, and then into garments and finished goods. As textile growth became more difficult, entrepreneurs started producing plastic products. At first polythene and polystyrene were injection-moulded. Plastic flowers were a growth sector, before tailing off in favour of plastic toy production. The electronics industry grew through the 1960s and 1970s, starting with assembly of components mostly sourced in Japan, for example, to make a radio set, and progressing into more value-added products such as televisions and computer components. In the 1970s wig manufacturing would account for 8% of all exports, before market trends moved from human to synthetic hair. Increasingly, capital was deployed to services, such as tourism and financial services.

It was truly the invisible hand that was directing these investment flows. Entrepreneurs or businesses would manage the life cycle of investments. At each stage these private investors would be efficient without state involvement. They would search out profitable investment opportunities, test and trial and then build capacity as their plans were delivered. They would manage these investments tightly, moving to higher value-added products and introducing more advanced technology. And as the opportunity faded, they would liquidate the business and extract what capital they could for investment elsewhere.

This powerful investment cycle would in turn produce good returns, which could be re-invested in new opportunities and create further growth.

LOW TAXATION

Cowperthwaite's successors have maintained Hong Kong's low tax levels. As a free port, Hong Kong has no sales tax, and very limited duties. Income tax had been introduced in 1939 to contribute towards the costs of World War II. It was a contentious debate and the governor felt that he could not impose an income tax using the government majority on the Legislative Council but needed the support of locally appointed members. Eventually, a compromise was agreed, with a 10% tax rate, separately calculated for salary, property income and businesses, all with a very large number of exemptions. Very few people would end up paying tax, but the precedence that local support was needed would limit the government's ability to raise taxation.

After another very heated debate after the war, the 10% rate was retained. The British government had pushed the governor to set the rate at 25%, given that the Atlee government in the UK had set a standard tax rate of 45%, with the highest rate being 92.5%. The governor wisely advised London that the 10% rate was already a stretch and resisted its advice. Given how much reconstruction was needed in Hong Kong many thought that the rate would need to rise. But, with a rapid recovery, tax revenues soon recovered and in fact were creating surpluses.

The Financial Secretary who successfully oversaw the reconstruction, Geoffrey Follows, made the case for higher taxation in 1950, despite government finances looking suspiciously healthy. But using his authority and the fear of the effects of the Korean War, he managed to get the rate increased to 12.5% (Monnery 2017).

Cowperthwaite was able to push the tax rate up to 15% in 1966, on the back of an unusual set of circumstances. The economy had slowed, and with lower than expected tax revenues there was a very unusual deficit. The tensions with China and the Cultural Revolution also weighed heavily. Cowperthwaite proposed this small increase because he believed that, with the increasing demand for social spending, government finances needed to be restructured to take a slightly higher share of output. But he was keen to keep tax rates low in order that private investment should continue to flourish.

His successors have held the tax rate at 15% ever since. Overall government revenues remain around or below 20% of GDP: similar to Singapore, but much lower than most countries. About a quarter of government revenue is linked to a service provided, a quarter comes from the tax on business profits, a quarter from taxes on salaries and investment income, 15% from land taxes and 10% from stamp duty. Sales tax, tariffs, duties and capital gains taxes are insignificant.

Cowperthwaite believed that it was very important for tax rules and structures to remain stable to help individuals and companies plan their futures. There can be few better examples of a stable and simple tax code as has existed in Hong Kong over the last half century or more.

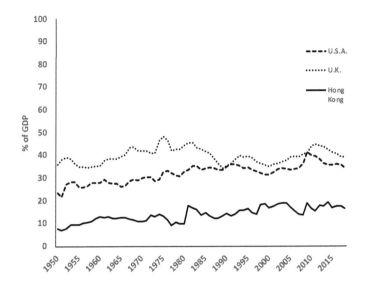

Figure 14. Government spending as % GDP 1950–2018 (Source: ukpublicspending.co.uk, usgovernmentspending.com; Hong Kong statistics 1947–1967, Censtatd.gov.hk, author)

The combination of limiting government revenues to between 15% and 20% of GDP, and also of targeting a budget surplus, creates a very strong envelope as to what government expenditure could be. Whilst spending had slightly increased as a proportion of GDP, it has remained well below that of other countries such as the US or the UK.

BUDGET SURPLUSES

Successive financial secretaries have adopted a conservative approach to fiscal policy, the result of which has been that in nearly every year the government has enjoyed a surplus. This is a marked policy difference with almost all other countries, who have been running budget deficits for decades. Instead of a national debt, there is a reserve fund to cover future spending; today this is worth over 40% of GDP and would cover more than two years of government spending.

It is a far cry from when Cowperthwaite arrived in Hong Kong in 1945. At that point the government had no assets and no income. There was no likelihood that the London government would provide any significant support, and so the then financial secretary, Geoffrey Follows, knew his recovery plans would need to be self-financing. Largely due to the cash balances in Cowperthwaite's department, they were. But the government learnt that it was deeply uncomfortable to not have a cushion that could cover shortfalls in difficult years. And so, a *modus operandi* developed where revenue items were conservatively forecast for future years, and all spending commitments were estimated in full and required to fit within the revenue forecasts. In practice, revenues tended to outdo forecasts and spending was usually well below forecast. The resultant surplus was then reserved for future years.

This story was repeated throughout Cowperthwaite's decade as deputy financial secretary and his subsequent decade as financial secretary. Not surprisingly the local members of the Legislative Council saw the pattern and demanded that the government spend more. The government resisted any acceleration of spending. They were committed to increasing government spending year-on-year effectively into perpetuity but saw no benefit in doing that oscillating between deficit and surplus. Why not build in a margin that would remove the chance of a deficit and any subsequent need for an austerity program?

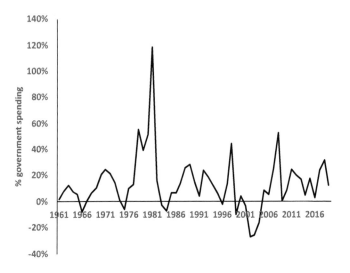

Figure 15. Hong Kong budget surplus as % of government spending 1961–2019 (Source: Censtatd.gov.hk)

So, Cowperthwaite ducked and dived to explain why in any particular year it was not sensible to dramatically increase expenditure, whilst also spending more and more each year. The resultant increase is government spending per capita was phenomenal. In 1960 government spending was around $600 per capita in inflation- and purchasing-power-adjusted international dollars. Today, the government spending per capita stands at $12,000 on the same basis, representing a twenty-fold increase in spending per person.

SOCIAL SERVICES

In 1961 Governor Black outlined the government's approach to investing in a variety of social services such as education, healthcare, welfare and housing. He emphasized that he saw social spending as dependent on a strong economy:

> Our calculations we direct, we hope in a realistic and unsentimental way, to discovering how to fulfil our humanitarian role within the boundaries of this small geographical location, and within the limits which its size and lack of natural wealth impose on our capacity. We can only do what we have set out to do if we remain a going concern, and, to ensure this in our peculiar conditions, we depend on our ability to maintain confidence, to attract capital to our midst, to exercise the minimum of interference in legitimate economic enterprise, and to find and keep markets abroad for the goods which we make in the factories which give employment and a livelihood to the people.[103]

For the last 60 years the Hong Kong state has gradually increased provision of services. Between 1960 and today, Hong Kong's population has risen from 3.1 million to 7.4 million. Over that period educational enrolment has blossomed. In 1960 242 students received first degrees in Hong Kong, now over 100,000 students graduate each year.[104] Secondary student numbers have risen from 70,000 to over 300,000. A wide variety of vocational and adult qualifications have been introduced. The number of doctors has risen from around 1,000 to nearly 15,000, and dentists from 400 to 2,500. A number of new professions have emerged, including occupational therapists, physiotherapists and radiographers. There were 8,000 hospital beds in 1960, and now there are 40,000. Today nearly one million people receive some form of welfare support where there was minimal support in 1960.

Hong Kong has developed a very comprehensive package of social programmes. What distinguishes Hong Kong is that these were developed within a constrained budget. Service provision was introduced when it could fit within the fiscal framework of the government and its prioritization of investment.

THE HOUSING EXCEPTION

Most social services – healthcare, education and welfare – grew slowly but steadily. Housing would prove to be an exception, both in the level of government involvement and in its scale. Hong Kong is often portrayed as one of the most expensive housing markets in the world, and if you want to buy an apartment on Hong Kong Island, it is. But around half the population live in government-built apartment blocks, with a third of the population renting at very affordable rents, and the remainder having bought subsidized housing units.[105]

Figure 16. The need for safe housing (early 1960s)

This massive government intervention in the housing market had its origins in the Shek Kip Mei disaster of Christmas Day 1953. A fire raged through the shanty town, leaving more than 50,000 people, mostly recent immigrants, homeless and in need of help. The government quickly accepted that there was a public safety issue in the vast refugee camps where hundreds of thousands lived, as well as a humanitarian need. Governor Grantham initiated new legislation in 1954, setting up a housing authority to build very small, affordable, safe accommodation. Powers to close illegal settlements and to force resettlement were also adopted.

Figure 17. Newly constructed high-rise government housing (1965)

The initial housing units were very basic. A family of three could rent a 90 square foot apartment with communal bathrooms and toilets, with a small external corridor also used for cooking. These cramped, but low-cost, apartments were hugely in demand and there were soon long waiting lists to live in them. Each new generation of apartment blocks has provided larger and better-appointed housing. But the philosophy remains the same: to provide mass accommodation that has very affordable rents, but that also broadly covers its costs.

Cowperthwaite reviewed the housing programme in the mid-1960s after it had been running for a decade. By then the government had housed a million people and had plans to house 1.6 million more in the next six years. Cowperthwaite was keen to ensure that the programme would be self-financing and not require subsidy from general taxation, and that the programme did not drift into building more expensive units that should be provided by the private construction sector.

Today, the standard three-room apartment built for the Hong Kong Housing Authority is around 500 square feet and costs approximately US$100,000 to build.[106] With an average rent of US$210 per month it is perhaps not surprising that there is a three-year waiting list. Despite the residents being lower-income, the very low rents mean that the average rent-to-income ratio for residents is around 10%.[107] There will be many in London or New York who dream of such a situation. The genius of the Hong Kong public housing initiative is that has mass produced very low-cost housing, which produces around 3% return on government investment, and which has left an active private construction market. The government has used its land reserves strategically to enable this enormous intervention in the housing market.

CHAPTER SIX

1997 AND THE BASIC LAW

In 1997 the UK lease on the New Territories came to an end, and although the actual island of Hong Kong had been ceded in perpetuity to the UK, the government did not believe it was defensible or economically viable to retain it alone. Therefore, the whole of Hong Kong was returned to Chinese sovereignty. Negotiations on this handover had been continuing in the background for 20 years, and in 1990 the Basic Law was agreed that would allow 'one country, two systems' for 50 fifty years between 1997 and 2047. The Basic Law had a number of clauses that protected Hong Kong's economic philosophy for the years ahead. Several articles committed Hong Kong to free trade and to retaining a business-friendly setting for international trade and finance. Article 107 guaranteed financial prudence and limited the growth of government spending to the overall growth of the economy. Article 108 identified Hong Kong's low-tax policy as the benchmark for future policy decisions

THE RESULTS

In the 60 years after Cowperthwaite and Guevara established the economic direction of their two economies, two very different societies have emerged. Cowperthwaite laid the foundations for what is now the best example of a free market economy that exists in the world today. He and his successors largely resisted the temptation to become a more mixed economy with a larger role for the state. Guevara established an economy with almost complete government ownership of the means of production, and very broad and deep state economic planning. His humanistic form of centralized communism is also a relatively pure and rare example of its type.

In terms of results, the difference in the evolution of GDP per capita was enormous. In the late 1950s both economies had a GDP per capita of around $4,500 in today's money. By 2018 Cuba had slightly more than doubled its GDP per capita to around $9,000 per person. But Hong Kong had reached $64,000 per capita. This was seven times the level of Cuba and exceeded that of the UK.

Other measures confirm the very large difference at the physical level too. Hong Kong consumes four times as much electricity per person as Cuba. It has six times as many mobile phones per person, and more than thirty times as many broadband subscriptions. Cuba has 30 personal computers per thousand people, versus 600 for Hong Kong.[108]

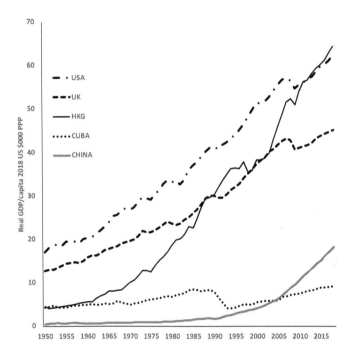

Figure 18. GDP per capita 1950–2018 (Source: Maddison Project Database, version 2018)

And the gap between Hong Kong and Cuban living standards is even greater at the level of household consumption. Hong Kong invests a much higher proportion of its GDP in investment: 22% versus 10% of a much smaller number for Cuba. Cuba's government spends over 30% of GDP, versus around 10% for

Hong Kong. The net result is that household consumption is 67% of Hong Kong's GDP, even after substantial investment, but only 57% of Cuba's. On this basis Hong Kong has a consumption per capita of $43,000 versus Cuba's $5,000. And even that may overstate the incomes in Cuba, given the complex and inefficient distribution system and the complexity of the two-tier currency.

EQUALLY POOR, UNEQUALLY RICH

Guevara and Cowperthwaite were concerned that prosperity should benefit society generally, not just a few oligarchs. As always, they differed in their approach as to how to achieve this. In Cuba incomes were controlled by the state, and the dispersion of income tightly managed, with each job having a salary set by the state. In Hong Kong there was no control on incomes at any level, with the market determining the resulting distribution. Cowperthwaite believed that economic growth would raise incomes with greater wealth for all:

> We hear much today about the danger of rising wages as if wages were the price of a commodity or a raw material. I suggest that we should look at rising wages from the point of view of the receiver as well as that of the payer and what it means to him. Furthermore, I myself welcome increasing wages which result by ordinary economic processes from the pressure of economic growth on our resources of labour, because they help to ensure both maximum export prices and the most productive use of our scarce resources; and at the same time redistribute more fairly our growing national income.[109]

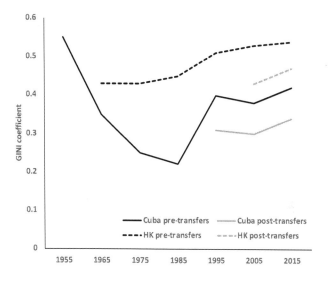

Figure 19. Inequality in Cuba and Hong Kong (Sources: Censtatd.gov.hk, Ferriol Muruaga (2001), Brundenius (1979, 1984), Mesa-Lago and Pérez-López (2005), Domínguez et al. (2013), Corrales (2012))

In development economics there has been a trend to argue that the right objective is not just growth alone, but growth and reduced inequality. The most widely used measure on inequality is the Gini coefficient: zero indicates perfect equality, and one perfect inequality. There are data issues, particularly for Cuba, which rarely provides the data to calculate it.* There are also many ways to calculate and interpret Gini coefficients, of which perhaps the most important is whether to include taxation and

---

* The Hong Kong government has provided the Gini coefficient annually, but only in recent decades. The Cuban government only sporadically provides income distribution data, and the last Gini coefficient calculation was in 2000. Various academics have tried to fill the gap, and their work is reflected here.

transfers.* On a post-tax, post-transfer basis Cuba has a Gini co-efficient of around 0.34, which is similar to Japan or the UK, but higher than that of Denmark or Sweden. Hong Kong is around 0.47, similar to Singapore, with both amongst the highest in the world.

Historically, Hong Kong has had high, and somewhat rising inequality as exemplified by their Gini coefficient. Cuba had a very high level of inequality under Batista (with a Gini of over 0.55), which fell rapidly after the revolution as the government dictated income levels, and as savings were effectively sequestered. In the last two decades inequality has significantly risen in Cuba, driven by two factors: dollar remittances from the US and *cuentapropistas*, who work in the small private sector.

Cuban emigrants, primarily in the US, sent money to relatives still in Cuba. In the early 2000s this ran at around $1 billion a year. With Obama's lifting of restrictions on transfers to relatives this surged to over $5 billion annually (on a GDP of around $80 billion).† In addition, there are around 600,000 who now work in one of the 181 permitted private jobs, mostly in the service sector, with some being able to generate income in US dollars.[110] Others have made use of a change in law that allows the rental of private accommodation, casa particular, or the opening of private restaurants. These trends have created a new strata of higher income households.

---

* For example, Gini coefficients can be calculated for individuals or households, can be adjusted for household size and composition, for all or just the economically active, before or after tax, before or after transfers, etc. And there is a tendency for Gini coefficients to be higher in richer, more urban, more service-based economies.

† Under Trump the US Treasury Department has banned large transfers from October 2019 and this will no doubt reduce inequality.

But was Cuba's lower Gini coefficient of any benefit to the poorest in society even before it started to rise to European levels? Today, the lowest decile of earners in Hong Kong receive $6,400 of income annually, compared with the average employee receiving $23,000. In Cuba the average salary is around $400 per annum, with a doctor earning around $600. These phenomenally low numbers are simultaneously accurate and misleading. Local wages are paid in local peso (CUP), which the government states are worth one convertible Cuban dollar (CUC). However, the market rate is that one CUC is worth 25 CUP. For any purchase that requires US dollars or convertible currency (such as travelling), wages are very, very low. But it is alleviated by some local goods being priced in local peso.

This is complicated to adjust for, as can be illustrated by examining the price of the humble egg in the two economies. In the US, eggs sell at around 20–25¢ each. In Hong Kong, anyone can buy as many eggs as they like for about 40 US cents per egg. Eggs in Hong Kong are quite expensive because they are largely imported, and the cost of running a supermarket (rent and labour costs) is high. So far, so simple. In Cuba you can buy five eggs per month on the ration-book system (if they are available) for less than 1¢ per egg (paying in local peso converted at market rates to US cents). A further five eggs can be purchased on rations at 4¢ per egg. Members of the Revolutionary Armed Forces (FAR) or the Ministry of the Interior (MINIT) have an additional allocation of ten eggs at 2¢ each. Markets run by the Youth Labour Army may sell additional eggs at around 6¢ per egg. On the black-market eggs sell at around 17¢ each.[111]

It is obviously rather complicated to make the multitude of adjustments necessary to understand the net effect on purchasing power income of all these government interventions. But it is perhaps safe to say that, for any normal basket of goods that includes internationally sourced products, the richest decile in Cuba is poorer than the poorest decile in Hong Kong. We also know that during the Special Period, and at other times, many Cubans faced starvation, with very many households teetering on the brink of subsistence. The effective subsidy through rationing and provision of services means that the standard of living is somewhat higher than the official data suggests, but it is still a very poor country indeed.

Cuba's experience raises important questions about the issue of income inequality and measures such as the Gini coefficient. How beneficial has it been for Cuba to have a lower Gini coefficient than Hong Kong? How much extra inequality would be worth having for increased growth for all? Is the recent increased Gini coefficient in Cuba, coming as it does from remittances and the beginnings of limited entrepreneurial activity, to be welcomed or not?

UNEMPLOYMENT

Cuba and Hong Kong have both considered unemployment to be deeply undesirable. But whereas the Cuban government has seen it as its role to manage unemployment directly, the Hong Kong government has not intervened directly. Unemployment in Hong Kong has largely resulted from the time needed to absorb large flows of immigration, economic fluctuations and the frictional unemployment as one sector declines and is replaced by another. For most of the post-war period, Hong Kong unemployment hovered around 2%.

It is much more difficult to get an accurate picture for Cuban unemployment. Officially, the unemployment rate has generally been low, but data is sporadic and questionable. Given the government's role as near-universal employer, it has frequently permitted disguised and hidden unemployment and under-employment to exist. State firms have continued to employ workers who have no jobs to do, or jobs that are only part-time, with the government providing sizeable subsidies for industries to maintain employment levels, or to provide training and alternative jobs. For example, when the Soviet sugar subsidy was withdrawn, the Cuban government used the Sugar Price Compensation Fund to provide 1.4 billion pesos to prevent redundancies between 2001 and 2003 (Hagelberg and Alvarez 2006). The armed forces headcount has been used to absorb unemployment. And the level of female participation, which is materially lower in Cuba than in Hong Kong, has also been a way to limit official unemployment. The subsidies needed to allow businesses to carry unemployed workers on their books are expensive to maintain, and more recently the liberalization of the self-employed sector has also helped limit the number unemployed.

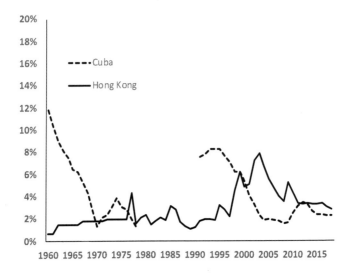

Figure 20. Unemployment rates in Cuba and Hong Kong (Sources: World Bank, ILO, Mesa-Lago (1981), ECLAC, Censtatd.gov.hk)

Both Hong Kong and Cuba have been conscious of the need to constrain the level of unemployment, and both have had some success in controlling the blight of unemployment. The Hong Kong government has followed its laissez-faire approach, facilitating a benign economic environment, but leaving it to private firms to create employment. The Cuban government has intervened directly, and often expensively, to create employment or at least disguised employment.

One advantage enjoyed by Hong Kong is the small distances involved. If a business closes, or an employee moves job, they are likely to suffer little dislocation. Almost everywhere in Hong Kong is within an hour's commute. In many bigger economics the difficulty of moving house and family can result in higher unemployment. Cuba lies in-between. Havana is a large and concentrated capital. But travel times from regional towns to other towns or the capital are prohibitive.

MIGRATION

An interesting measure of the success of an economy is whether people are attracted to it, or conversely if its residents wish to flee. For both Hong Kong and Cuba there have been huge flows of migrants between the 1960s and today. But whereas in Hong Kong the flow has been inwards, in Cuba it has been outwards. On a net migration basis, approximately 2 million people immigrated into Hong Kong, mostly from communist China. An almost identical 2 million people have emigrated from Cuba, mostly heading to the United States. With populations of just over 7 million in Hong Kong and 11 million in Cuba, these flows have materially impacted growth rates and use of resources, such as housing. In both situations the flow has been towards economic freedom.

The movements of people do occur in waves, but net migration over 60 years has averaged about 30,000 people a year into Hong Kong, and 30,000 a year out of Cuba.

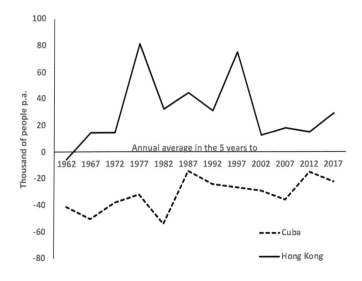

Figure 21. Average annual net migration (Sources: United Nations Population Division, World Population Prospects)

In the first few decades of its industrialization, Hong Kong crucially attracted a number of Chinese entrepreneurs who played a vital role in its commercial success. There were all the benefits of first -generation immigrants building success in their new home. Equally, many leaving Cuba were skilled workers or managerial or professional. Cuban Americans have enjoyed success in every field, with the one million second generation American Cubans doing even better than their parents in terms of education, income and the like. One of the side-effects of Cuba allowing large numbers of disaffected people to leave is that it has been a safety valve for dissent. If people feel strongly enough, there is a way to escape from the Castro regime, and so internal pressure to reform is reduced.

There are those who argue that ethnicity and culture play a key role in bringing prosperity to an economy, with some cultures more suited to delivering economic growth. But the history of Hong Kong and of migration counters this view. For many decades Hong Kong, with its Chinese population, boomed when mainland China languished. In Singapore and Taiwan, ethnic Chinese populations also succeeded. When China turned to market solutions, these same populations suddenly delivered great economic growth. Some claim that it was the combination of British and Chinese cultures in Hong Kong that created success.[112] But again, the success in Singapore, Taiwan and post-reform China suggest otherwise. Cubans in Cuba have delivered a paltry level of economic growth over the last 60 years. And yet Cuban Americans run large companies, make fortunes and, on average, have higher incomes than other Hispanic Americans. In Cuba many have seized the chance to be self-employed. It would seem that for Hong Kong and China there was not a predetermined outcome driven by culture. At least for these two economies it would seem that in the right context the population is capable of creating growth and prosperity.

TRADE

Hong Kong is the most open economy in the world, with exports and imports equalling around 190% of GDP.[113] For comparison, the equivalent number for Germany is 45% of GDP. Cuba is, by circumstance and design, much less integrated into the world economy, with exports and imports accounting for about 15% of GDP. This, combined with the very different sizes of their economies, means Hong Kong exports are worth around $700 billion versus $14 billion for Cuba.

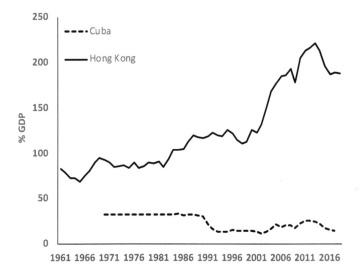

Figure 22. Exports as a % of GDP (Source: World Bank)

Cuba's exports are comprised of sugar, cigars, nickel, tourism and the services of medical staff abroad. The once mighty sugar industry remains the main export but delivers only around $0.5 billion per year. Hong Kong still exports textiles, manufactured goods and tourism but increasingly its key exports are complex machinery, instrumentation, financial and other services.

Being so open, the Hong Kong economy requires domestic firms to compete against companies from America to Zambia. There are no quotas or tariffs to provide protection. This requires companies to quickly shift from businesses where they are losing competitive advantage to those where they can build advantage. Cuba manages imports and exports through the state with quotas, tariffs, currency regulations and licensing requirements. Not surprisingly Cuba has developed few new streams of export earnings. The temporary protection afforded to domestic sectors appears to have come at a material cost in terms of competitiveness and adaptability.

GOVERNMENT SPENDING

The Hong Kong government raises taxes and other revenues equivalent to around 23% of GDP[114] compared with Cuban government revenues of 58% of GDP.[115] Hong Kong typically runs a budget surplus and saves a part of their revenues into reserves, and this has recently been around 5% of GDP. Cuba has been running a budget deficit of nearly 10% of GDP.

A significant difference is the spending on social security and welfare transfers, and after allowing for these, government final spending in Hong Kong is around 15% of GDP, a number that has remained fairly constant since the end of World War II. In most European economies, government spending has triple that share of GDP, with Switzerland being the nearest example of a low-government-spending economy. Cuba's spending is over 30% of GDP. Because of Hong Kong's greater prosperity, the total level of government spending is about the same in the two economies (around $65 billion), and on a per capita basis Hong Kong spends about three times as much despite it having a much lower share of GDP.

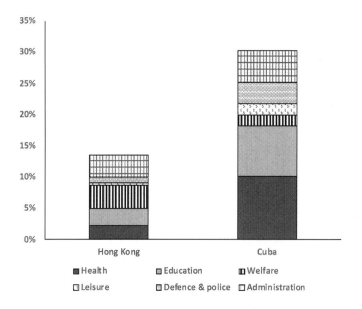

Figure 23. Government spending as % GDP (Sources: Censtatd.gov.hk, ONEI)

Spending on healthcare and education is the biggest driver of these differences. Cuba spends over 10% of GDP on healthcare, versus 2% for Hong Kong. And on education the difference is 8% versus 3% of GDP.

Hong Kong and Cuba have a similar number of hospital beds per capita. But Cuba has over four times as many doctors per person, although a significant number of these may be seconded abroad. Hong Kong has been increasing doctor numbers, but only slowly, and it still has fewer doctors per capita than the US or the UK.

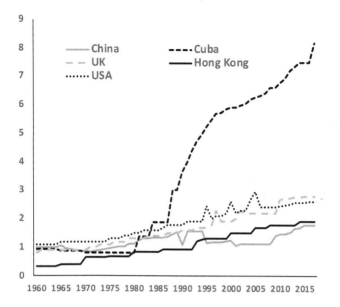

Figure 24. Number of doctors per 1,000 people (Sources: World Bank, WHO, OECD, Censtatd.gov.hk)

There is considerable academic debate as to the efficacy of the huge investment in healthcare by Cuba. It has been politically popular but has required high levels of taxation. The debate centres on the great progress regarding longevity that was already being made in pre-revolutionary Cuba. If this was an established trend, then the big gains in longevity after the revolution might have happened anyway. Furthermore, Hong Kong had similar improvements with very low levels of government health spending.

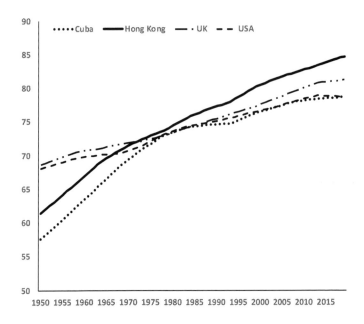

**Figure 25. Life expectancy in Cuba and Hong Kong in years
(Source: United Nations Population Prospects)**

The last quarter century also poses some intriguing questions.
Cuba, with huge investment, has tracked the longevity of the
much richer but equally high-spending USA. But it has underperformed the improvements seen in the UK, and even more
dramatically underperformed Hong Kong. Today's citizen of
prosperous but low-healthcare-spending Hong Kong can expect
to live more than five years longer than the average Cuban.[116]

A similar picture emerges in education. Cuba has achieved very
high levels of literacy, similar to those in Hong Kong. Both require children to attend nine years of education. Cuba has only
9 pupils per teacher at the primary school level, versus over 14
in Hong Kong. It is similar at secondary level: 9 pupils per secondary school teacher in Cuba, and 20 in Hong Kong. A similar

proportion of students go on to study at a tertiary level. Various bodies such as UNESCO regularly commend the level of educational attainment in both Cuba and Hong Kong.

The huge relative investment in education in Cuba appears to be very popular, but again there are questions as to its efficacy and to whether some of those funds could have been better used. Some economists have put human capital at the centre of economic development, but there is scant evidence from these two economies that education alone is a driver of growth. If it were, Cuba would have outperformed Hong Kong. As well as not delivering GDP, Cuba's education system does not deliver a proportional quantity of high-level academic output. Honk Kong produces 275 technical or scientific journal articles per million inhabitants, versus Cuba's 24.[117]

The very different models for healthcare and education hark back to the days of Guevara and Cowperthwaite. Guevara saw extensive spending on education and health as morally right. What would have surprised him was that it has not translated into higher levels of prosperity. Cowperthwaite was more conditional in his support for healthcare and educational spending. He saw these as good things, but he also saw the low tax levels that allowed an entrepreneur to invest in a textile factory as a good thing. And so, he traded investment in welfare against investment in wealth creation. Cowperthwaite was widely criticized for his frugal stance when in office, but with the benefit of hindsight his tempered approach seems to have combined progress on education, health and prosperity.

ECONOMIC FREEDOM

Not surprisingly, Cuba performs very badly in rankings of economic freedom. In the Heritage Foundation index of economic freedom, Hong Kong has typically been the highest ranked economy over the last quarter century, and Cuba one of the lowest ranked. Similar results come from other surveys, such as the annual Economic Freedom of the World report.[118]

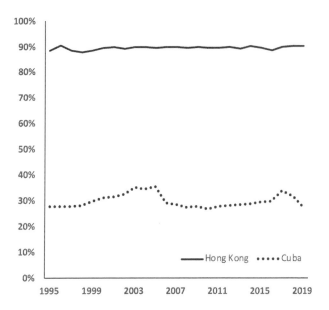

Figure 26. Index of Economic Freedom (Source: The Heritage Foundation)

Cuba trails Hong Kong on all the dimension measured, but is particularly weak on high effective taxation and on the freedom to make investments.

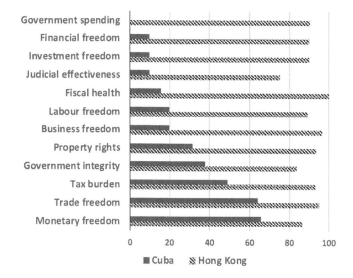

Figure 27. Economic freedom scores by category (Source: The Heritage Foundation)

The *Economist* magazine produces a Democracy Index, in which Hong Kong is classed as a flawed democracy and Cuba as authoritarian. Hong Kong has historically performed well in terms of civil liberties and political culture, but has low scores in categories affected by Hong Kong's limited democracy and partial elections. Cuba again scores towards the bottom of the rankings.

The World Bank sponsors work to classify the ease of doing business within different economies. Hong Kong has consistently been classed as 'very easy to do business' and has been ranked in the top five such economies (out of 180+) alongside Singapore, New Zealand, South Korea and Denmark.[119]

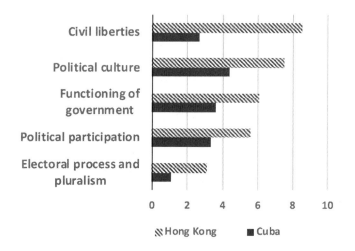

Figure 28. Democracy Index for Cuba and Hong Kong (Source: The Economist)

HAPPINESS

Anyone visiting Cuba quickly realizes that the Cuban people seem a lot more cheerful than one would expect given the economic data. And it is easy to understand that living in a warm, cultured Caribbean island with an over-developed healthcare and education sector certainly compares well with the communism that exists in North Korea or in the old USSR. In general happiness or satisfaction scores tend to rise with GDP per capita, although the relationship is very loose and tends to plateau at higher income levels. The survey questions are notoriously difficult and can give inconsistent conclusions, and there are limited data points for Hong Kong and Cuba, and very few where they are both in the same data set.

The World Happiness Report registered that in 2006 Hong Kong scored only slightly higher than Cuba in terms of life satisfaction. Part of this may be cultural. Latin America and the Caribbean produce much higher scores than the world average, whereas in Southeast Asia scores are lower and cluster around the mean. Confusingly, some other surveys produce different results: the World Value Survey reports that Hong Kong has very high scores of people who say they are 'very happy' or 'happy'. They do not include Cuba in their survey, but rank Hong Kong alongside the UK and US for happiness. Conversely, a 2016 Gallup world poll ranked Hong Kong very low in terms of life satisfaction, whereas Taiwan was the happiest country, with Singapore coming second. Nonetheless, the divergence in happiness between Hong Kong and Cuba may be much lower than the divergence in prosperity, and more research needs to be done to confirm the difference and identify its causes.

There is work to be done to clarify the data and assess causes. Various hypotheses have been advanced for low levels of happiness, such as the cost of living, lack of democracy and identity. The key question for economic policy will be whether there is something Hong Kong can do to improve life satisfaction through economic means. Some hypothesize that the root of any Hong Kong unhappiness may instead reside in issues of identity. The people of Hong Kong have had to contend with dramatic change. From city state to part of the world's largest nation; from creating nearly 20% of China's GDP in 1997 to now less than 3%; from colony to province; from British to Chinese; from striving to prosperous; from economically anxious to politically and socially anxious; and many other challenges too.

Survey scores are not the only relevant data. Another satisfaction measure is the level of immigration and emigration. As we saw, around 20% of Cuba's population were sufficiently dissatisfied to leave the country, sometimes at great personal risk. And about 25% of Hong Kong's population are people who have chosen to move to Hong Kong. One paradox is the level of protest, some violent, that has occurred in Hong Kong in recent years. It appears as if this is symbolic of people who want to defend the status quo and are fearful of change, in particular a loss of Hong Kong's way of life. Perhaps the fears and worries that underlie this make it hard to fully enjoy the material prosperity.

The more detailed questions in life satisfaction surveys also reinforce the unique way that Cuba provides satisfaction. A 2006 poll showed 74% of Cubans had confidence in their healthcare system (versus 42% across Latin America) and 78% were satisfied with their education system (versus 59% for Latin America).[120] Impressively, 60% believe Cuban colleges to be better than those in other countries. Most significantly 96% believe healthcare is accessible for anyone regardless of their economic situation (versus 42% for Latin America) and 98% (versus 52% for Latin America) feel that is true for education. When asked whether Cuba is a good environment for child development, 96% say yes (versus 46% for Latin America). But when the survey turned to work, the scores for Cuba plummeted. Only 26% were satisfied they had the freedom to choose what to do with their lives (versus 80% for Latin America). Only 42% (versus 77%) say people can get ahead by working hard.

A recent unauthorized 2014 poll of Cubans reinforced this view.[121] Where 68% were satisfied with their healthcare system and 72% satisfied with the educational system, and only 19% were satisfied with their economic system. People understood the economic issues facing Cuba: 34% of people receive money from family members abroad, with most of this needed to cover everyday expenses; 55% would like to emigrate and 70% would like to own their own business. Given these views, it is not surprising that 58% have a negative view of the communist party, and 53% are dissatisfied with the political system.

SUMMARY

Some stark messages emerge from the economic performance of Hong Kong and Cuba since Cowperthwaite and Guevara embarked on their economic policies. Hong Kong has created incredible prosperity, moving from relative poverty to become one of the richest economies that has ever existed on Earth. It has been a phenomenal achievement. By contrast, Cuba has stagnated economically. Cuba has, however, dealt with some of the issues of alienation and exploitation that so exercised Guevara, and also positively supported education, welfare and healthcare.

But Cuba has paid a very high opportunity cost to deliver the gains that it has. The main cost has been economic, but it has also come in reduced freedom, mass emigration and frightening fragility to shocks. On an economic front, Hong Kong appears to have hardly put a foot wrong decade after decade. In terms of societal cohesion Hong Kong could have perhaps accepted a slight increase in government spending to support key needs, but they would have been right to worry that too great a level of spending may have hit growth rates in due course.

Politically, both economies have come to a difficult juncture. Hong Kong is struggling as to how it can retain its freedoms as a politically autocratic China exerts more control. And Cuba will need to find an accommodation with its powerful neighbour if it wants to pursue some of its recent attempts to liberalize parts of its economy.

The primary purpose of this book, however, is not to look forward, but rather to note the incredible difference in performance between Hong Kong and Cuba in the six decades since the start of the natural experiment in the early 1960s. Wherever the two economies should go from here, it would be a great shame if their story over this remarkable period was not remembered and studied in the decades ahead.

JOURNEY'S END

Cowperthwaite would retire from his role as Financial Secretary in 1971, and then spend a decade as a part-time advisor to Hong Kong–based investment bank Jardine Fleming. This allowed him to travel in Asia, and to return to Hong Kong for the horse racing and to play golf. In 1981 he fully retired and settled down to a quiet life of golf, travelling and reading in St Andrews.

He was succeeded by Philip Haddon-Cave, who had worked as his deputy. Haddon-Cave was more open than Cowperthwaite, and more willing to share data. But he retained most of the same economic beliefs and policies. In 1995 Donald Tsang became the first Chinese financial secretary, and his term straddled the 1997 handover.

Cowperthwaite was in Hong Kong for the handover ceremonies in 1997. The last governor, Chris Patten, met him and reportedly remarked; 'so, you are the architect of it all'. Cowperthwaite died in January 2006, aged ninety, having seen Hong Kong transformed from the barren island he had arrived in 60 years earlier, in 1945. Three weeks after his passing, his wife died, at the age of 88.

Guevara would become increasingly frustrated with the challenges involved in administering socialism in Cuba and would yearn for a return to fomenting revolution. Despite having had four children with his second wife, Aleida March, in the five years preceding 1965, his main concern on leaving Cuba to spread the revolutionary message seems to have been his relationship with Castro. He had clearly come to see him as a father figure. But in early 1965 Guevara travelled to Africa to explore options.

In April, Guevara and a dozen Cuban fighters would join revolutionary forces in the People's Republic of the Congo. It was not a success and the US-backed government easily contained the rebel forces. Guevara's health was deteriorating and, suffering from dysentery and acute asthma, he decided that the others should leave, and he should fight on alone until he was killed. He was persuaded to join the others, and in November the six remaining fighters and Guevara left the People's Republic of the Congo.

The future for Guevara looked bleak. In his own words, Congo had been a 'story in failure' (Anderson 1997). Castro had publicized his 'farewell letter', in which Guevara severed all ties with

Cuba and renounced his citizenship in order to fight for 'revolution throughout the world'. Guevara had only meant this knowledge to become public after his death, so returning to a role in Cuba would have been humiliating. Instead, Guevara made clandestine visits to Cuba, Africa and Europe.

He eventually decided to return to fight in Bolivia, arriving there in November 1966. He started with around 50 well-armed guerrilla fighters, but soon problems emerged. As in People's Republic of the Congo , Guevara found it difficult to work productively with local rebels. In addition, the government had active assistance from the US and the CIA, and he did not get support from the peasants, who may even kept the government well informed of the guerrillas' movements. He suffered crippling asthma attacks that required him to be moved around on a donkey. It was a dark time.

In October 1967, Bolivian troops surrounded the rebel force in Yuro ravine. In the subsequent action, Guevara was wounded twice and threw down his weapon and surrendered, shouting 'Do not shoot me! I am Che Guevara and I am worth more to you alive than dead' (Anderson 1997). He was held captive overnight at a local school whilst the troops waited for orders. The following morning the Bolivian president ordered that Guevara be killed. One soldier volunteered to execute Guevara. He fired several shots, hitting his arms and legs but failing to kill Guevara, who writhed on the ground. The soldier would end up shooting Guevara nine times before he died.

REFLECTIONS

The story of the Hong Kong and Cuban economies over the last 60 years is one of drama, complexity and consequence. It is a story of humans shaping their societies in complex ways, blending abstract ideas, knowledge and experience in dynamic and multifaceted environments. The adaptability of the human species has meant that many have found happiness, or sadness, in their life journeys in both societies. But what different journeys they have been. One has seen relative poverty transformed into incredible prosperity, with the responsibility for the outcome being widely shared and with little by way of a safety net. The other has seen an intense effort by a central elite to improve the lot of the least fortunate, but at a huge cost to longer term wealth. Whichever route you would yourself have taken, there is a dignity in the human endeavour involved in both attempts.

The main claim of this book is that the Hong Kong and Cuban economies over this period deserve to be more studied than they are. They provide a valuable, possibly unique, natural experiment in contrasting how very distinct economic policies affect growth and prosperity. Both are comparatively pure examples of their

chosen economic philosophies: one based on free markets, laissez-faire, competition and an open economy; the other based on
state ownership, state planning, constrained inequality and limited openness. With the prevalence of mixed economies today,
these unalloyed cases can provide insight. Helpfully, the stability
of economic policy pursued by Hong Kong and Cuba over six
decades and the magnitude and consistency of the difference in
resulting performance give us confidence that we are observing
systemic differences.

Drawing detailed lessons from two data points has its challenges.
But this comparison can provide some hypotheses about economic policy and prosperity, and these are listed below. Addi-
tionally, any model of economic growth would need to be able
to validly explain the success of Hong Kong and the failure of
Cuba. The comparison can also provide some heuristics, or rules
of thumb, about policy levers. The relatively unadulterated examples of capitalist Hong Kong and communist Cuba can provide some boundary conditions for discussing economic policy
and its results: state versus private ownership; planned versus
free markets; directed versus dispersed investment decisions;
self-directed versus rationed consumption; the motivation of
self-interest versus societal interest; open versus closed economies; etc.

ECONOMIC POLICY MATTERS

For many people, for much of the time, economic policy is dry,
obscure and technical. Economists have done an extraordinary
job of turning a vital subject into a boring and inaccessible one.
And politicians often reduce economic policy to soundbites and

token initiatives at election time. And yet it is the key determinant of the lives that we, our families and our descendants live. The famous economist, Sir Roy Harrod, claimed that:

> Economic growth is the grand objective. It is the aim of economic policy as a whole.[122]

Prosperity brings not only material richness but also longevity, opportunity, education and more. It shapes the society in which we live, both enabling and constraining what we may do and who we may be. A society that is not engaged with making choices about economic policies has subcontracted out its future direction.

Cuba and Hong Kong show how different choices about economic policies have affected millions. Between them they represent the boundaries of potential futures – few economies have done better than Hong Kong, and few have done worse than Cuba. Few have adopted the classical economics model more comprehensively than Hong Kong, and few the Marxist model more meticulously than Cuba.

The people of Hong Kong and Cuba had limited say in the policies adopted. The resulting consistency of policy over the decades is an enormous advantage for this comparative study. But such an imposition cannot work in a modern democracy. Indeed, it may not work much longer in Hong Kong or Cuba. For those that believe both in democracy and that economic policies drive prosperity and the shape of society, there is an obvious gap in the public discourse about how we direct economic policy.

Nowadays, at least four groups need to play a role: experts, political representatives, the population and the media. Experts and technocrats have greatly extended their influence over the decades but there are doubts as to their expertise, their alignment with society as a whole and their ability to communicate effectively. Political representatives face challenges of trust, economic competence and who they are serving. Many people feel unqualified and unempowered to participate in economic policy. And yet they must make the ultimate decisions. The media is a double-edged sword. At its best, its ability to inform and educate can help close the gaps identified here. At its worst, it is a force of ignorance, sensationalism and discord.

Cowperthwaite and Guevara spent a great deal of time communicating their economic visions and explaining their thinking, even though they did not face elections. Others in the past have increased society's economic acuity, for example: FD Roosevelt and his radio talks, Margaret Thatcher's speeches, Milton Friedman's television programmes and Lee Kuan Yew in describing Singapore's model. Maybe the countries that do the best job of raising their collective ability to discuss, debate and resolve economic policies will have greater prosperity in the decades ahead.

IT'S NOT JUST THE ECONOMY, STUPID

Bill Clinton's 1992 presidential campaign against George H. W. Bush famously led on the idea that economic performance drove political success or failure. Maybe in an ideal world a population would debate and discuss economic policy, make a choice and then implement it. Then they would review progress and results and nudge the tiller one way or the other. In reality, particularly in less economically advanced countries, the process is less well thought out, less rational and less incremental.

But, in many situations, the population may not be masters of their own economic destiny. In Cuba, Batista came to power via a coup and embarked on an economic policy of crony capitalism. He was replaced by a rigid communist state. As Guevara acknowledged: 'non-revolutionary forces indeed helped smooth the road for the advent of revolutionary power'.[123] Guatemala voted for liberalism and reform, but instead got a coup and an autocratic crony-capitalist economy. After the Japanese occupation, in 1945 Hong Kong was almost liberated by the communist Chinese forces, but instead reverted to a British colony. In 1997 China regained sovereignty over Hong Kong without any process of consent, and today the people of Hong Kong protest in order to retain their economic and political freedoms. In Korea if you live in one part of the country you live in a capitalist society, in the other a communist one.

Even where you have some power, it is constrained. It may be possible to remove a failing government but only get a very constrained choice as to what follows. Cuba is a good example. The anti-Batista movement successfully overthrew a crony-capitalist regime. It was even initially replaced with a broadly liberal government that was probably what the majority would have wanted. But soon government was in the hands of a small group who had the power to impose an ideology that suited them. Choices are constrained, and even more so in volatile situations. There are many in Hong Kong who would like an economically laissez-faire, politically liberal democracy. But it seems that that choice is not on the available list of options. It is possible that protest succeeds in bringing down an existing government only to get something worse.

In the countries discussed in this book, economics and politics do not split in a tidy way. And the relationship between political process and institutions is also not straightforward. Democracy was limited both in economically successful Hong Kong and unsuccessful Cuba. Cuba's political structure has not come under much challenge despite its economic failure, whereas Hong Kong's economic success has not prevented challenges to the political settlement. For many countries successful development is more than economic progress alone. The ability to vote to end one government and to select freely another with an alternative set of economic policies is a great privilege. Throughout the history of mankind very few people have had that power.

THERE IS A WINNING ECONOMIC FORMULA

For any government interested in increasing the prosperity of its people, if given the choice solely between copying the economic policies of Hong Kong or of Cuba, there could be only one rational choice. In two generations Hong Kong has moved from relative poverty to become one of the richest nations on Earth. Cuba has moved from being one of the richest countries in Latin America to become one of the poorest.

The economic policies that Hong Kong deployed are reasonably easy to identify, in part because they have been used consistently and clearly for over 60 years. The main elements are:

> a. the rule of law;
> b. the enforceability of property and contract rights;
> c. an open economy with free trade and capital movements;
> d. free markets;

e. private enterprises making their own decisions on where and how to compete;

f. private enterprises risking their own capital deciding where investment should be allocated;

g. government industrial intervention limited to dealing with monopolies, market failures and investing in public goods and services;

h. conservative fiscal and monetary policy;

i. low tax rates to attract and retain capital and to provide surpluses that can be invested for growth;

j. government spending targeted on the greatest needs and managed efficiently, given low taxes and an aversion to deficits.

It is informative to contrast this list of policies with that John Williamson described as the Washington Consensus (Williamson 1990). Williamson attempted to synthesize what was viewed as effective development strategies by the Washington-based institutions (the World Bank, the IMF and the US Treasury). Williamson argued that the 1970s reliance on industrialization and import substitution had been replaced by three big ideas: the market economy, openness and macroeconomic discipline (Williamson 2002). The ten policy areas where he thought there was consensus were:

a. property rights;

b. trade liberalization;

c. liberalization of foreign inward direct investment;

d. financial liberalization;

e. deregulation (easing barriers to entry and exit);

    f.   privatization (into competitive markets);

    g. tax reform (broad tax base with modest marginal rates);

    h. fiscal discipline (towards pro-growth and pro-poor expenditures);

    i.   re-ordering public expenditure priorities.

There is a striking similarity between the two lists. If there is a difference, it is not in direction but in degree. For example, Hong Kong's fiscal discipline is exceptional; its openness to trade is deep; its commitment to light regulation pervasive. For those in Hong Kong over the last 60 years, the economic policy approach is deeply ingrained and of constant relevance.

The example of Hong Kong would suggest that we know quite a lot about how to engender prosperity. The issue is that we are not willing to follow that path.

IS COMMUNISM AN ECONOMIC DEAD END?

If Cuba is representative of the effect of communism on an economy, it is perhaps not surprisingly that the communist model has been in retreat. In the early 1960s there were nearly 40 countries that combined communist political power and a centrally planned economy, but most have moved away from that model.[*] Today, two remain: North Korea and Cuba.

---

[*] Russia (1922–1991), Ukraine (1922–1991), Armenia (1920–1991), Azerbaijan (1919–1991), Estonia (1940–1991), Latvia (1940–1991), Lithuania (1940–

The purely economic story of North and South Korea is not dissimilar from that of Cuba and Hong Kong. Between the end of the Korean War in 1953 and the early 1970s, the trend in GDP per capita of the two parts of Korea was similar, with North Korea rebuilding the pre-war economy and exporting to the Soviet, Chinese and non-aligned blocs. But then the two economies took very different paths. North Korea moved to a philosophy of national self-reliance, called *Juche*, isolationism, totalitarianism and a personality cult around the Kim family. For the next four decades the economy stagnated. In South Korea the 1970s saw a move away from earlier protectionism and a focus on growing export markets. Democracy was extended, and measures of economic freedom were introduced. Today, the real GDP per capita in North Korea is below $2,000; the anaemic growth in the early period petered out after the move to *Juche*. South Korea by contrast enjoys an income per head of around $40,000.

1991), Belarus (1922–1991), Georgia (1922–1991), Kazakhstan (1936–1991), Kyrgyzstan (1936–1991), Moldova (1940–2009), Tajikistan (1929–1991), Turkmenistan (1925–1991) , Uzbekistan (1924–1991), Mongolia (1924–1992), Yugoslavia (1943–1992), Bulgaria (1946–1990), Albania (1946–1992), Poland (1947–1989), Romania (1947– 1989), Czechoslovakia (1948–1990), Hungary (1949–1989), East Germany (1949–1990), Yemen (1967–1990), Somali Democratic Republic (1969–1991), People's Republic of the Congo (1969–1992), Ethiopia (1974–1991), Mozambique (1975–1990), Benin (1975–1990), Angola (1975–1992), Madagascar (1975–1992), Afghanistan (1978–1992), Grenada (1979–1983), Kampuchea (1979–1991), Burkina Faso (1984–1987).

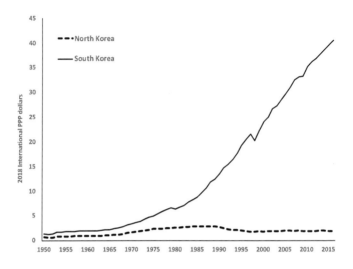

Figure 29. GDP per capita for North and South Korea (Source: Maddison Project database, 2018 version)

Cuba and North Korea's dismal economic performance, and the collapse of most communist economic systems, provides a clear warning for any country tempted to emulate the model of comprehensive economic and political communism. That said, there is a material difference between Cuba and North Korea. North Korea has used its very limited economic resources on military spending. It is hard to imagine anyone choosing to live in that country. Cuba, on the other hand, has used its limited resources on over-investing in education, healthcare and ensuring employment even in downturns. This is the result of the priorities that were set by Guevara after the revolution, which still exist today.

An interesting response to the economic dead end of communism comes from the three countries that retain a unitary communist party in political power but have largely abandoned the centralized economic planning of the 1960s. The most significant of these is China, with Vietnam and Laos following a similar line. Rather than being an example of the success of socialism, China provides another useful example of how moving away from state ownership and planning delivers prosperity. And the unresolved question that it poses is whether economic liberalism and political autocracy can be a stable mix.

Modern communist China came into being in 1949 after the Civil War. There was extensive collectivization, nationalization and centralized planning under Mao. Mao also launched initiatives designed to harmonize society, such as the Hundred Flowers Campaign, the Great Leap Forward and the Cultural Revolution. As we have seen, Guevara was impressed with these attempts to harness the consciousness of the worker, but they may have been less welcome to the millions that died through starvation or persecution. Economically Mao's reign was not successful, with a growth rate over nearly two decades of less than half of that of Hong Kong.

In the late 1970s, Mao's successor, Deng Xiaoping, became the 'architect of modern China'[124] crafting 'socialism with Chinese characteristics', which attempted to blend the unitary power of the communist party and the modernization of the Chinese economy. The Four Cardinal Principles listed the issues that could not be debated: continuing on the socialist path; upholding the people's democratic dictatorship; not questioning the sole leadership of the Communist Party of China; and accepting the ideology of the Communist Party. The question was whether these principles could accommodate economic liberalization. Beijing was of course intimately familiar with the economic success of Hong Kong, demonstrating the power of the market and of private enterprise. With its anachronistic colonial form of government, it suggested that economic liberalism could be combined with political autocracy.

Deng led the economic liberalization that he hoped would avert another quarter century of the meagre growth seen under Mao. China started a wave of privatization, dismantled the planning structure in favour of markets and opened the economy to foreign investment and to pursue exports. In the late 1970s agriculture was de-collectivized and trade was encouraged. In the 1980s private firms were allowed, and in the 1990s and 2000s many state-owned enterprises were privatized. Today, state-owned enterprises account for only 5% of industrial firms, 20% of employment and 25% of output. The remaining state-owned enterprises tend to be in the utility or heavy industry sectors.

Deng supported the establishment of Special Economic Zones in mainland China, which enjoyed special free-market policies and more flexible government rules. Shenzhen in Guangdong Province, just beside Hong Kong, was the first of these, set up in 1980. It allowed Beijing to test and understand how economic polices worked, particularly in the 'Chinese context'. Shenzhen has boomed since then, growing from a population of 300,000 to over 10 million.

Deng turned nationalization and planning from objectives into tools, suggesting that:

> Planning and market forces are not the essential difference between socialism and capitalism. A planned economy is not the definition of socialism, because there is planning under capitalism; the market economy happens under socialism, too. Planning and market forces are both ways of controlling economic activity.[125]

Whereas China's real GDP per capita grew at below 2% per annum in the quarter century under Mao, it has grown at more than 6% per annum since Deng's reforms started. Not surprisingly the Chinese Communist Party has been careful to brand the approach as a form of socialism, first as 'socialism with Chinese characteristics', and later, by Jiang Zemin, who succeeded Deng as paramount leader, as 'socialist market economy'. Of course, China has nowhere near a Hong Kong or Singapore level of economic freedom but it is a very long way from the communist model that continues to be used in Cuba.

Given the communist model has largely failed and is, in practice, in retreat, it is odd that there are those who want to resurrect it. Perhaps it is the romance of lost causes, or virtue signalling, or a tactic to obtain power, or maybe the lack of knowledge and understanding as to economic history. In this area at least economic practice and theory align. Robert Solow argued that:

> Marx was an important and influential thinker, and Marxism has been a doctrine with intellectual and practical influence. The fact is, however, that most serious English-speaking economists regard Marxist economics as an irrelevant dead end.[126]

CRONY CAPITALISM MAY NOT BEAT MARKET COMMUNISM

It is a great mistake to simplify the economic policy choice to capitalism versus socialism. Anyone looking at the economies of Cuba, North Korea and China would quickly realize that they are very different, despite often being described as communist.

As we have seen, Cuba has largely been a centrally planned, state-owned economy with some self-employment at the edges. Cuba and North Korea have had the dismal economic performance that seems to result from that policy mix.

But China's economic policy is very different from that. State ownership is lower than in many Western democracies. And, being largely export driven, China has forced its industries to compete globally, not be protected domestically. It has used many elements of market economic policy to create prosperity for hundreds of millions of citizens. At least for now this free-market economic approach has sat alongside an autocratic political system. Only time will tell whether this is a stable policy mix. For now, however, it is clear that communist political structures that combine with state ownership and central planning are not the same as those that use free-market economic policies.

Equally, the story of Hong Kong's success versus the communist economic policies of Cuba should not give false succour to champions of capitalism. Hong Kong's is a very pure form of free-market capitalism. It is not the same as the crony capitalism that is increasingly practiced in Western democracies.

In post-war Hong Kong there was little value in lobbying the government for favourable regulations or protectionism. As an open economy, Hong Kong's companies were forced to compete in the global market and, when they were disadvantaged, exporters from other countries quickly destroyed weak business models. Machinery and components would flow in from Japan, commodities and products requiring land from Asia, and products requiring cheap, low-skilled labour came first from China and then other low-cost countries. And if a company's business model became uncompetitive, there were no government funds available to support that model or slow its creative destruction.

The worst examples of crony capitalism are also combined with corruption, as with the Batista regime in Cuba. But capitalism can tend towards cronyism without severe corruption. *The Washington Post* has estimated that there are nearly 14,000 registered lobbyists in Washington, and *The Guardian* has reported that there are nearly 30,000 lobbyists in Brussels. The European Parliament keeps a partial list of lobbyists and estimates that there are over 11,000 lobbying organizations with 82,000 lobbyists, of which 7,000 have access to Parliament.[127] Few can doubt that this huge investment is an attempt to obtain economic rent, to be granted privileges that increase a firm's share of existing wealth without creating new wealth. And one of the key problems is that once one competitor starts to engage in such behaviour it is rational for others to follow to ensure they are not disadvantaged.

There is a whole field of economics – public choice economics – which challenges the widespread assumption that politicians and administrators are neutrally trying to improve society. Instead, many believe that they too are trying to maximize their own utility, even when it is at the expense of society more broadly. A classic example is for a politician to attempt to obtain protection for local companies employing local voters so that they may be re-elected. Or they may get campaign financing as a *quid pro quo* for lobbying.

Socialism provides little attraction to those in a genuine free-market capitalist system such as Hong Kong. In fact, there are many willing to protest to defend its unique economy from greater Chinese influence. But, in a clash between crony capitalism and socialism, the relative attractiveness is far less clear.

Market competition facilitates improvements in productivity and the optimal allocation of capital. State ownership and state planning is a poor substitute for the dynamic forces of the market, and so leads to a decline in prosperity. But so too does interference with market mechanisms through corruption and cronyism. For anyone interested in prosperity, the choice between a Hong Kong and a Cuban economic model is straightforward. But if the choice is between two mixed economies, one with sporadic state intervention and the other with sporadic crony regulations, then the route to prosperity becomes rather less clear cut.

WHY DO MARKET POLICIES OUTPERFORM?

Why has its policy mix worked so well for Hong Kong? Economic growth comes from two sources: operating efficiency and resource allocation. Without adding extra resources, it is usually possible to increase output over time from a wide range of improvements using new ways of working, gaining experience, learning-by-doing, increasing specialization, optimizing distribution, refining pricing, using machines more efficiently and the like. Hong Kong has utilized its resources very effectively to date. With domestic and international competition, entrepreneurs and business owners need to be efficient to succeed, and so they have the incentive to look for opportunities to become more productive. A good example of this was the textile industry in the 1960s. British and US textile firms found it hard to understand why they were unable to meet Hong Kong costs and prices. After many studies, and with great reluctance, they came to realize that the Hong Kong companies were simply more efficient. They unceasingly looked for ways to be more profitable and found ways to improve sourcing, cost controls, labour scheduling, number of shifts, machine downtime and so on.

They had a very strong incentive to do this. If they found an improvement in their business model, it increased their profits. In fact, in most industries the world price of any product falls each year as someone in the industry finds an improved way of operating and passes it on to their customers. That means that some improvements are necessary in all competitors just to allow their profits to stand still. Hong Kong's open economy ensured that Hong Kong producers were fully subject to global competition, ensuring all business owners are continuously looking for improvements to plug the gap from structurally falling prices.

In Cuba, enterprises were protected from these forces, and indeed it was often not in an individual's interests to identify and deliver improvements. As well as this incentive problem, the lack of market prices, and in particular the ability of prices to change to encourage improvements and decisions, meant that firms could react slowly, if at all. Business organization also plays a key enabling role. In Hong Kong a supervisor in a business would be encouraged and incentivized to look for improvements; knowing something about the economics of the business and its operations, the focal point of making improvements would be quite decentralized. In Cuba, by contrast, the plan largely prevailed, with trade-offs being made at a very centralized level, where operating and financial information could not be explored in a detailed and accurate way. In a market-based system there are normally thousands, or millions, of people involved in delivering progress. In centralized systems this opportunity is often wasted, and even though Guevara tried many routes to circumvent this issue and empower those closest to the work being done, the system largely blocked this.

The second main cause of progress in Hong Kong was the remarkable way in which entrepreneurs and firms allocated their resources, in particular their investments. As opportunities arose to deploy capital profitably, firms would enter new markets, be that textiles, enamelware, wigs, electronics, plastics, insurance, banking, property development or a host of other industries. And as the opportunity closed, they would withdraw that investment, redeploy it and close the previous business. This dynamic allocation of capital was hugely successful, and the government was clear that it would not stop new investments being made, nor protect old investments from being liquidated.

MARKET DYNAMISM BEATS STATE STASIS

Another way of looking at the above phenomenon is that markets tend to set the pace of change for all participants, whereas state planning can stop the forces of change. One of the attractions of a socialist approach is to maintain the status quo and slow or eliminate the need to adapt to change, for a stated reason of saving jobs, for example. But the suspension of time leads to the suspension of progress. Capitalist markets are unsympathetic to all the difficulties in transitioning an economy from one set of industries to another, but it rarely makes sense to forgo the longer-term benefits of such changes. Better to provide support to those affected than to opt out of market progress.

The dynamic nature of markets and the stasis caused by state planning is evident in the stories of Hong Kong and Cuba. Where Hong Kong's output today looks completely different from the 1960s, in both category and size, Cuba has hardly changed. Hong Kong's economy has evolved continuously, while Cuba has been rigid and slow to adapt. Ironically, Cuba had a clear aspiration, from the time of Guevara onwards, to create a modern economy, less dependent on sugar. But it was Hong Kong, which had no central view as to how the economy should evolve, that actually delivered progress and change.

CUBA STILL HAS A SURPRISING APPEAL

Given the dismal performance of Cuba's economy relative to that of Hong Kong, it is odd that there are those who champion the Cuban approach. But there are a number of rational reasons why they might.

Firstly, Cuba chose its path not versus a free-market model, but rather versus Batista. His crony capitalism hit both the expected long-term growth rate of the economy and the distribution (or rather non-distribution) of rewards within it. Secondly, some people will rightly have a short time horizon, and a redistribution towards them now may well be worth a slower longer-term growth rate, which they may not benefit from. Thirdly, the Cuban government was shrewd to invest heavily in education and healthcare. For many, being unable to afford an operation or to provide education to their children must be a dreadful prospect. Many on lower incomes may be able to adjust their budgets for small expenditures but have no realistic way to cover the eventuality of a healthcare crisis or an educational cost. For these people, it may be entirely rational to accept a lower long-term growth rate in exchange for that fear being removed. It is surely this trade-off that has led to free and subsidized healthcare and education in many capitalist countries.

Beyond these economically rational perspectives, there will be those who would prefer philosophically to live in a poorer, more equal society. Of course, that is a continuum, and the key question is how much more extra equality one wants to pay for by increased relative poverty. The Cuba and Hong Kong examples suggest that the price can be very high indeed and last for generations. At the extreme of these groups are the Marxists, who claim that one person's prosperity comes at the expense of another's poverty. The story of Hong Kong gives little support to the idea that one group has succeeded at the expense of another, even in that unequal society. Rather, it is Cuba that has needed to use coercion and violence, and to lose nearly 20% of its people to emigration, in order to impose its policies.

For those who weigh equality and reduced alienation highly, surely the answer lies closer to the Nordic model, which combines free-market, competitive, privately owned enterprise with high levels of tax and redistribution. This model avoids the inefficiency inherent in the state-owned model, which harms productivity and poorly directs new investments.

The flipside of the point above is how difficult it can be to convince people how effective capitalism is at delivering progress and prosperity. It requires differentiating the free-market version from the crony one. And it requires a proper time perspective. The news is filled with noisy commentary about this quarter's GDP forecast, or the closure of a plant. Meanwhile, productivity improvements, or new investments, go unnoticed. It is hard in the context of this barrage of negative triviality to step back and consider how the dynamism of capitalism drives prosperity.

Often the political system can encourage and reward taking action rather than trusting in the market system. This is exacerbated by a tendency for markets and capitalism to be blamed for the failures of government. Cowperthwaite did not have to get elected, and, even for him, following the correct course, as he saw it, was very challenging. It is surely government's job to ensure competition, create regulations and enforce the law. When they fail to do so they undermine capitalism. And it is, of course, the role of politics to balance the need to ensure the health of the golden goose of capitalism with the desire to provide government- and taxpayer-funded services. As in Hong Kong and Cuba, the decisions on balancing these needs are critical to developing society and the economy in tandem.

ECONOMIC POLICY IS A HUMAN STORY

Those who have lived through the last 60 years in Hong Kong and Cuba have seen two very different economic stories play out. Both have been remarkable journeys. Someone born in the developing economy that was Hong Kong in the 1950s will have recently retired in one of the world's most prosperous. Income per capita has increased more than fourteen-fold, and Hong Kong has become materially richer than its old mother country, Britain. It took Britain around 170 years to increase GDP per capita from around $4,000 to $40,000. Hong Kong completed that same feat in less than 60 years. Hong Kong provides an inspiring story of how skilled administration and economic policy making can combine with entrepreneurial and business talent to facilitate an economic miracle. Anyone interested in economic growth and prosperity must surely look to this impressive case study.

Over the same period, someone born into the developing Cuba of the 1950s will have retired seeing modest economic progress over their lifetime. And they will have lived through some difficult times. Some of their friends and family are likely to have emigrated. Sometimes they will have been short of food and had little by way of economic resources. When the Soviet Union disintegrated in the early 1990s, Cuba's GDP per capita was no better than it had been at the time of the revolution. Since then, modest growth has returned, driven in large part by greater political openness, expatriate remittances and self-employment. However, on almost every dimension Cuba's economy compares poorly with that of Hong Kong. With major changes possible in both economies, now is an ideal time to explore the contrasting fortunes of this extraordinary natural experiment.

Cuba's relative success is that, compared with the nearly 40 communist command-economy countries that existed in the early 1960s, it is one of only two that survive, and in reality the only one that has any vestige of normality. Not to have disappeared is a strange measure of success. Many argue that its survival is due to its focus on health and education, and its attempt to address the issues that triggered the Cuban revolution – alienation, exploitation, colonialism, identity, dignity and the like. These issues may not have been solved by Cuba, but equally they have not been entirely solved by capitalism. Perhaps the answer is to combine the economic engine of free markets with a more sophisticated definition of what constitutes economic success.

Economic policy is the very human story of policymakers attempting to improve their societies. To understand how economic policy is crafted, and to improve that process we need to put humans at the centre of this story. The key participants have prejudices, world views and interests that they bring to policy formulation. And in practice, ideas create decisions, decisions lead to actions, and actions yield results in an economic labyrinth, where the expected does not always happen. Human responses to uncertainty and changing environments can be wise and fast or stubborn and slow. The study of economic policy should provide policymakers with a clear understanding of the economics and of the decision making involved.

And the end results of effective policymaking will be visible in the competitiveness of the wealth-creating enterprises in that economy. For both businesses and policymakers several real-world questions are key tests of economic vitality. Are our industries competitive? Do they earn above the cost of capital? Are they responsive to changing costs, prices and markets? Is technology applied to get superior returns? Do people freely choose to invest in our businesses? Are people and capital continuously being moved from lower to higher return opportunities? Economic policies that allow these questions to be answered in the affirmative are the basis of prosperity.

 The aim of this book is to encourage debate about macroeconomic policy, its relationship with wealth creation in the business sector and the link between the economy and society more generally, particularly over the long term. The greater our collective knowledge, the more likely we are to achieve future success and prosperity in our societies.

ENDNOTES

[1] Airports Council International, 2018

[2] Airports Data Net, 2017. Centre for Aviation estimate 2015 passenger numbers as only 4 million.

[3] Emporis

[4] www.fosca.com

[5] Maddison Project Database, version 2018 (Bolt *et al.* 2018). The data for real GDP per capita in 2011 purchasing power parity international dollars has been inflated to 2018 international dollars.

[6] Discussion between Ed Leamur (author of *Macroeconomic Patterns and Stories*) and Russ Roberts. Econtalk. 4 May 2009

[7] *New York Times,* 4 May 1961

[8] *The Economist,* 5 May 1962

[9] Hansard, 24 February 1960

[10] Hansard, 24 February 1960

[11] Mr Barton, Hansard, 16 March 1960

[12] Mr Barton, Hansard, 16 March 1960

[13] Speech by Fidel Castro, 17 July 1959

[14] Guevara, E., 1960. Speech to an assembly of works in Havana, 18 June 1960. Published in *Obra Revolucionaria*, No. 11, 1960

[15] 'One year on: Hong Kong bookseller saga leaves too many questions unanswered'. *South China Morning Post.*, 29 December 2016

[16] Guevara, E., Speech to an assembly of works in Havana, 18 June 1960. Published in. *Obra Revolucionaria*, No. 11 1960

[17] Maddison Project Database, version 2018

[18] 'The real lesson of Hong Kong', speech by Milton Friedman at Mandel Hall, University of Chicago, 14 May 1997

[19] Speech by Nelson Mandela in Cuba, 26 July 1991

[20] Comment by Walter Sauer, executive vice president of the Export-Import Bank, an arm of the US Treasury

[21] Author's discussions with family members

[22] Guevara, C. 2002. *Back on the Road.* Grove Press, New York

[23] 'Professor James Wilkie Nisbet: an appreciation', Alan Peacock, *Alumnus Chronicle,* Volume 61 (University of St Andrews, 1970)

[24] Monthly Report, DST&I, HKRS 170-1-551-1, September 1946

[25] See www.myersbriggs.org

[26] Guevara, E. 1965. Speech at the Second Economic Seminar of the Organisation of Afro-Asian solidarity. Delivered 26 February 1965 Translated, translated in *Che Guevara Speaks*, Pathfinder Press (Guevara 1967)

[27] *Marshall Lectures.* University of Cambridge, 1985

[28] Hong Kong Hansard, 26 February 1969

[29] Guevara, E., Speech to an assembly of works in Havana, 18 June 1960. Published in. *Obra Revolucionaria*, No. 11 1960

[30] Guevara, E., 1961. Speech at the Special Meeting of the Inter-American Economic and Social Council of the Organization of American States, Puenta del Este, Uruguay, 8 August 1961

[31] Guevara, E. *Obra Revolucionaria*

[32] Guevara, E. Interview with Jean Daniels 1964. Cited in Tablada Perez (1990)

[33] Guevara, E. 1963. *Reuniones bimestrales,* 21 December 1963 in *El Che en la revolucion cubana,* Vol. 6

[34] Guevara, E. 1965. 'Man and socialism in Cuba'. Letter to Carlos Quijano, editor of Marcha. Also printed in *Verde Olivo*.

[35] Guevara, E. 1965. 'Man and socialism in Cuba'.

[36] Hong Kong Hansard, 26 February 1969

[37] Hong Kong Hansard, 26 February 1964

[38] Hong Kong Hansard, 28 February 1968

[39] Guevara, E. 1965. 'Man and socialism in Cuba'.

[40] Guevara, E. 1965. Afro-Asian solidarity.

[41] Hong Kong Hansard, 24 March 1966

[42] Hong Kong Hansard, 30 March 1962

[43] Letter from Cowperthwaite to Kirkness, HKRS 163-1-2210, 20 March 1963

[44] Hong Kong Hansard, 29 March 1963

[45] Guevara, E. 1962. Balance sheet of the Punta del Este conference. *Marxist Review*, February

[46] Hong Kong Hansard, 30 March 1962

[47] Speech by Clement Atlee to the Labour Party Conference, Bournemouth, 11 June 1946

[48] Hong Kong Hansard, 27 February 1963

[49] Hong Kong Hansard, 30 March 1962

[50] Guevara, E. 1961. 'Cuba's economic plan'. People's University television episode broadcast 30 April 1961. Translated in *Che Guevara Speaks* (Guevara 1967)

[51] Hong Kong Hansard, 30 March 1962

[52] Guevara, E. *Obra Revolucionaria*

[53] Hansard, 24 March 1966

[54] Hong Kong Hansard 27 March 1968

[55] Hong Kong Hansard 28 February 1962

[56] Guevara, E. *Obra Revolucionaria*

[57] Guevara, E. *Obra Revolucionaria*

[58] Guevara, E. 1961. 'Cuba's economic plan'

[59] Guevara, E. *Obra Revolucionaria*

[60] Hong Kong Hansard, 27 March 1968

[61] Hong Kong Hansard, 30 March 1962

[62] Hong Kong Hansard, 27 March 1968

[63] Guevara, E.,. 1961. Cuba: exceptional case or vanguard in the struggle against colonialism? *Verde Olivio,* Issue 9, April. Translated in *Che Guevara Speaks* (Guevara 1967)

[64] Guevara, E. Cuba: exceptional case?

[65] Hong Kong Hansard, 9 October 1970

[66] Hong Kong Hansard, 24 February 1966

[67] Hong Kong Hansard, 24 February 1966

68 Guevara, E. 1963. May Day Speech at the Garcia Lorca Theatre, Havana, 30 April

69 Hong Kong Hansard, 30 June 1965

70 Hong Kong Hansard, 24 February 1971

71 Hong Kong Hansard, 29 March 1963

72 Hong Kong Hansard, 30 March 1967

73 Hong Kong Hansard, 26 March 1969

74 Guevara, E. 1960. Notes for the study of the ideology of the Cuban revolution. *Verde Olivio*, Issue 8, October 1960. Translated in *Che Guevara Speaks* (Guevara 1967).

75 Hong Kong Hansard, 27 March 1968

76 Guevara, E. 'Cuba's economic plan'

77 'File more' by Cowperthwaite, HKRS 163-9-281, 28 August 1969

78 Hong Kong Hansard, 25 March 1970

79 See Friedman and Friedman (1998)

80 *The Guardian*, Alex Singleton, Obituary, 8 February 2006

81 Guevara E. 1959. Yugoslavia, en pueblo que luncha por sur ideas. *Verde Olivo*, 26 November

82 Guevara, E. 1960. Ideology of the Cuban revolution

83 Guevara E. 1960. *Intervención en el Ciclo de Conferencias del Banco Nacional,* 20 October

84 Kennedy J. F. 1961. State of the Union Address

85 World Trade Organization

86 Guevara, E. Speech on 17 September 1960. Published in *Che Guevara Speaks* (Guevara 1967)

87 Census of the Republic of Cuba, 'Education in pre-revolutionary Cuba'

88 Guevara, E. 1961. 'Cuba's economic plan'

89 UNESCO 1998. *Primer Estudio Internacional Comparativo sobre Lenguaje, Matemática y Factores Asociados en Tercero y Cuarto Grado*. Santiago: Laboratorio Latinoamericano de Evaluación de la Calidad de la Educación.

90 Penton, M. 2018. Cuba set to kick off the new school year with a shortage of 10,000 teachers. *Miami Herald*, 22 August

[91] BBC News 2019. The hidden world of the doctors Cuba sends overseas, 14 May. Available at https://www.bbc.co.uk/news/uk-48214513

[92] Castro, F. 1970. Discurso en el X aniversario de la constitución de la FMC. *Granma Revista Semanal*, 30 August

[93] Castro, F. 1971. Speech to the workers in Chuquicamata. *Granma Weekly Review*, 28 November

[94] Castro, F. 1971. Speech at the Rio Verde sheep farm, Magallanes. *Granma Weekly Review*, 5 December

[95] Dorticós, O. 1970. Discurso en la inauguración de la Escuela de Cuadros del Ministerio de la Industria Ligera. *Granna.*, 16 September 1970.

[96] Castro, F. 1966. Speech on 28 September, reported in *Cuba Socialists* No. 62

[97] Hayek, F. A. 1945. The use of knowledge in society. *American Economic Review* 35(4), 519–530.

[98] Guevara, E. Puenta del Este, Uruguay

[99] Guevara, E. Puenta del Este, Uruguay

[100] Guevara, E. 1964. The Cuban economy: its past, and its present importance. *International Affairs* 40, 589–599

[101] *The Economist* 2018. New rules make it even harder to do business in Cuba, 8 December

[102] Whitefield, M. 2018. New Cuba regulations for private enterprise on the island have a long list of don'ts. *Miami Herald*, 2 August

[103] Hansard, 1 March 1961

[104] Censtatd

[105] HK Government 2015. Hong Kong: the facts – housing. Fact sheet, Information Services Department, August

[106] Reply by the Secretary of Transport and Housing, Prof. Anthony Cheung Bing-leung, to Hon Abraham Shek in Legislative Council., 12 April 2017

[107] Hong Kong Censtatd 2016. Population by census (Housing)

[108] Nationmaster

[109] Hansard, 9 October 1970

[110] *The Economist*. New rules make it even harder to do business in Cuba
[111] Torres, I. 2012. Dirty eggs for ordinary Cubans. *Havana Times,* 26 October
[112] Hampton, M. 2017. *Hong Kong and British Culture, 1945–97*. Studies in Imperialism Series. Manchester University Press
[113] World Bank Open Data
[114] Hong Kong Censtatd
[115] Cuba ONEI
[116] For further discussion of how prosperity and longevity interact, see Marin Tupy 2017. *Free markets have made the world a better place*, 17 October, Humanprogress.org
[117] National Science Foundation, Science and Engineering Indicators
[118] Data from the *Economic Freedom of the World: 2018 Annual Report*. The Fraser Institute, Canada
[119] World Bank. *Doing Business 2020,* Report.
[120] Gallup 2006. Gallup poll of Cuba, September. Reported in The Gallup Organization's Cuba ThinkForum
[121] Poll by Bendixen and Amandi on behalf of Univision Noticas/Fusion in collaboration with *The Washington Post* by Bendixen & Amandi. The survey of 1,200 Cubans took place in March 2014
[122] Harrod R., 1965. *Reforming the World's Money*. Macmillan, London
[123] Guevara, E. Cuba: exceptional case?
[124] "Faison, S. 1997. Deng Xiaoping is dead at 92: architect of modern China. *The New York Times,* 20 February
[125] Gittings J. 2005. *The Changing Face of China.* Oxford University Press
[126] Kliman, A. 2006. *Reclaiming Marx's 'Capital': A Refutation of the Myth of Inconsistency.* Lexington Books.
[127] LobbyFacts.eu

BIBLIOGRAPHY

Acemoglu, D., Johnson, S., and Robinson, J. A. 2005. Institutions as the Fundamental Cause of Long-Run Growth. In Aghion, P., and Durlauf, S. (eds.), *Handbook of Economic Growth*. Amsterdam: North Holland.

Álvarez de Toledo, L. 2010. *The story of Che Guevara*. London: Quercus.

Anderson, J. 1997. *Che Guevara: A Revolutionary Life*. London: Bantam Press.

Apostel, L., and der Veken, V. 1991 *Wereldbeelden. Van fragmentering naar integratie*. DNB/Pelckmans (transl. Aerts *et al.*, 1994 *World Views: From fragmentation to integration*. Brussels: VUB Press).

Backhouse, R. 2002. *The Penguin History of Economics*. London: Penguin.

Bernanke, B. 2002. Remarks at the 'Conference to Honor Milton Friedman', at the University of Chicago. Board of Governors of the Federal Reserve System, 8 November.

Blake, R. 1999. *Jardine Matheson: Traders of the Far East*. London: Weidenfeld & Nicolson.

Bolt, J., Inklaar, R., de Jong, H. and van Zanden, J. L. 2018. Maddison Project Database, version 2018. Available at https://www.rug.nl/ggdc/historicaldevelopment/maddison/releases/maddison-project-database-2018.

Bray, D. 2001. *Hong Kong Metamorphosis*. Hong Kong University Press.

Brundenius, C. 1979. Measuring income distribution in pre-and post-revolutionary Cuba/Avaluacin cuantitativa de la distribución de ingresos en Cuba en los perodos pre-revolucionario y pos-revolucionario. *Cuban Studies* 9(2), 29.

BIBLIOGRAPHY

Brundenius, C. 1984. *Revolutionary Cuba, the Challenge of Economic Growth with Equity*, Vol. 4. Boulder, CO: Westview Press.

Carlyle, T. 1841. *On Heroes, Hero-Worship, and the Heroic in History*. London: James Fraser.

Carroll, J. 2007. *A Concise History of Hong Kong*. Hong Kong University Press.

Castro, F. 1978. *Informe al I Congreso del PCC*. Instituto Cubano del Libro, Havana.

Chang, E. R. 1969. *Report on the National Income Survey of Hong Kong*. Hong Kong: Government Printer.

Cheung, G. 2009. *Hong Kong's Watershed: The 1967 Riots*. Hong Kong University Press.

Chou, K. 1966. *Hong Kong Economy: A Miracle of Growth*. Hong Kong: Academic Publications.

Collins, C. 1952. *Public Administration in Hong Kong*. London, New York: Royal Institute of International Affairs (published in cooperation with the International Secretariat, Institute of Pacific Relations).

Corrales, J. 2012. Cuba's 'equity without growth' dilemma and the 2011 *Lineamientos*. *Latin American Politics and Society* 54(3), 157–184.

Coyle, D. 2014. *GDP: A Brief but Affectionate History*. Princeton University Press.

Domínguez, J. 1978. *Cuba: Order and Revolution*. Cambridge, MA: Harvard University Press.

Domínguez, J., Pérez Villanueva, O. E., Espina Prieto, M., and Barbiera, L. 2013. *Desarrollo económico y social en Cuba: Reformas emprendidas y desafíos en el siglo xxi*. (Engl. Transl. E. C. Muñiz and S. Guardado). Mexico: Fondo de Cultura Económica.

Donnison, F. 1956. *British Military Administration in the Far East, 1943–46*. London: HMSO.

Dorn, J. 1998. *China in the New Millennium: Market Reforms and Social Development*. Washington, DC: Cato Institute.

Eltis, W. 1984. *The Classical Theory of Economic Growth*. London: Macmillan.

Endacott, G. 1964a. *A History of Hong Kong*. Oxford University Press.

Endacott, G. 1964b. *Government and People in Hong Kong 1841*. Hong Kong University Press.

Erikson, D. 2009. *The Cuba Wars: Fidel Castro, the United States, and the Next Revolution*. London: Bloomsbury.

Ferguson, N. 2003. *Empire: How Britain Made the Modern World*. London: Allen Lane.

Ferguson, N. 2008. *The Ascent of Money: A Financial History of the World*. London: Penguin.

Ferriol Muruaga, A. 2001. La réforme économique de Cuba durant les années 1990. *Alternatives Sud* 8(1) , 211–230.

Franklin, J. 2016. *Cuba and the US Empire: A chronological history*. New York: Monthly Review Press.

Friedman, M. 1953. *The Methodology of Positive Economics: Essays in Positive Economics,* University of Chicago Press.

Friedman, M. 2006. Why money matters. *Wall Street Journal*, 17 November.

Friedman, M., and Friedman, R. 1998. *Two Lucky People: Memoirs*. University of Chicago Press.

Gonzalez, M. 2004. *Che Guevara and the Cuban Revolution*. London: Bookmarks Publications.

Goodstadt, L. 2005. *Uneasy Partners: The Conflict between Public Interest and Private Profit in Hong Kong*. Hong Kong University Press.

Goodstadt, L. 2006. Government without Statistics: Policy-Making in Hong Kong 1925–85, with Special Reference to Economic and Financial Management. HKIMR Working Paper 6/2006.

Goodstadt, L. 2007. *Profits, Politics and Panics: Hong Kong's Banks and the Making of a Miracle Economy, 1935–1985*. Hong Kong University Press.

Goodstadt, L. 2013. *Poverty in the Midst of Affluence: How Hong Kong Mismanaged Its Prosperity*, revised edition. Hong Kong University Press.

Goodstadt, L., and Mao, Z. 1972. *Mao Tse Tung: The Search for Plenty*. London: Longman.

Gott, R. 2004. *Cuba: A New History*. New Haven, CT: Yale University Press.

Guevara, E. 1960. Notes for the Study of the Ideology of the Cuban Revolution. *Verde Olivio*, Issue 8, October (translation in *Che Guevara Speaks*, Pathfinder Press 1997).

Guevara, E. 1961a. Cuba: Exceptional Case or Vanguard in the Struggle Against Colonialism. *Verde Olivio,* Issue 9, April (translation in *Che Guevara Speaks*, Pathfinder Press 1997).

Guevara, E., 1961b. *Cuba's Economic Plan*. People's University television episode broadcast, 30 April (translation in *Che Guevara Speaks,* Pathfinder Press 1997).

Guevara, E. 1967. *Che Guevara Speaks: Selected Speeches and Writings,* Lavan, G. (ed.). Atlanta, GA: Pathfinder Press.

Guevara, E., 1996. *The Motorcycle Diaries*. London: Fourth Estate.

Guevara, E. 2009. *Reminiscences of the Cuban Revolutionary War*. London: Harper Perennial.

Guevara, J., and Vincent, A. 2017. *Che, My Brother*. Cambridge, UK: Polity Press.

Haavelmo, T. 1944. The probability approach in econometrics. *Econometrica*. 12 July: Supplement, pp. 1–115.

BIBLIOGRAPHY

Hagelberg, G., and Alvarez, J. 2006. Historical Overview of Cuba's Costs of Sugar Production 1959–2005. Factsheet, University of Florida.

Hambro, E. 1955. *The Problem of Chinese Refugees in Hong Kong* (report submitted to the United Nations High Commissioner for Refugees). Leyden: A. W. Sijthoff.

Hamilton, G. 1969. *Government Departments in Hong Kong, 1841–1969.* Hong Kong: Government Printer.

Hansen, J. 2019. *Young Castro: The Making of a Revolutionary.* New York: Simon & Schuster.

Hartwell, R. 1995. *A History of the Mont Pelerin Society.* Indianapolis, IN: Liberty Fund.

Hempel, C., and Oppenheim, P. 1948. Studies in the logics of explanation. *Philosophy of Science* 15(2), 135–175.

Hook, S. 1943. *The Hero in History: A Study in Limitations and Possibility.* Boston, MA: Beacon Press.

Hopkins, K. (ed.). 1971. *Hong Kong, the Industrial Colony: A Political, Social and Economic Survey.* Oxford University Press.

Horne, A. 1988. *Macmillan: 1957–1986.* London: Macmillan.

Horowitz, I., and Suchlicki, J. 2009. *Cuban Communism 1959–2003.* Piscataway, NJ: Transaction Publishers.

Hughes, R. 1968. *Hong Kong Borrowed Place: Borrowed Time.* London: Andre Deutsch.

Jao, Y. C. 1974. *Banking and Currency in Hong Kong.* London: Macmillan.

Jones, G. 2000. *Merchants to Multinationals: British Trading Companies in the Nineteenth and Twentieth Centuries.* Oxford University Press.

Keirsey, D. 1998. *Please Understand Me II: Temperament, Character, Intelligence.* Green Valley Lake, CA: Prometheus Nemesis Book Co.

Keynes, J. M. 1936. *The General Theory of Employment, Interest and Money.* London: Macmillan.

Kolesky, C. 2011. Ernesto 'Che' Guevara: A Psychobiographical Study. Doctoral dissertation, Nelson Mandela Metropolitan University, Port Elizabeth, South Africa.

Lange, O. 1972. The computer and the market. In *Socialist Economics,* Nove, A., and Nuti, D. (eds.). London: Penguin Books.

Levy, D. M., and Peart, S. J. 2009. Soviet Growth and American Textbooks. SSRN Working Paper, 3 December. Available at http://dx.doi.org/10.2139/ssrn.1517983.

Li, K. 2012. *Economic Freedom: Lessons of Hong Kong.* Singapore: World Scientific.

Littlewood, M. 2010. *Taxation without Representation: The History of Hong Kong's Troublingly Successful Tax System.* Hong Kong University Press.

Lovell, J. 2012. *The Opium War: Drugs, Dreams and the Making of China.* London: Picador.

Ma, R., and Szczepanik, E. 1955. *The National Income of Hong Kong, 1947–1950.* Hong Kong University Press.

Macaulay, T. 1848. *The History of England from the Accession of James the Second.* Philadelphia, PA: Porter & Coates.

Malthus, T., and Gilbert, G. 1993. *An Essay on the Principle of Population.* Oxford University Press.

Marshall, A. 1916. *Principles of Economics. An Introductory Volume,* 7th edition. London: Macmillan.

BIBLIOGRAPHY

Mesa-Lago, C. 1978. *Cuba in the 1970s: Pragmatism and Institutionalization.* Albuquerque, NM: University of New Mexico Press.

Mesa-Lago, C. 1981. *The Economy of Socialist Cuba: A Two Decade Appraisal.* Albuquerque, NM: University of New Mexico Press.

Mesa-Lago, C., and Pérez-López, J. 2005. *Cuba's Aborted Reform: Socio-economic Effects, International Comparisons and Transitional Policies.* Gainesville, FL: University of Florida Press.

Meyer, D. 2000. *Hong Kong as a Global Metropolis.* Cambridge University Press.

Mill, J. S. 1848. *Principles of Political Economy: With Some of Their Applications to Social Philosophy.* London: John W. Parker.

Miners, N. 1987. *Hong Kong under Imperial Rule, 1912–1941.* Oxford University Press.

Mintz, S. 2004. *Sweetness and Power: The Place of Sugar in Modern History.* London: Penguin.

Monnery, N. 2017. *Architect of Prosperity: Sir John Cowperthwaite and the Making of Hong Kong.* London: London Publishing Partnership.

Morton, A 1938. *A People's History of England.* London: Victor Gollancz.

Newton, S. 2010. The Sterling Devaluation of 1967, the International Economy and Post-War Social Democracy, *The English Historical Review* CXXV, Issue 515, 912–945.

Nisbet, J. W. 1929. *A Case for Laissez-faire.* London: P. S. King & Son.

OECD 2017. General government spending (indicator). National Accounts (accessed on 27 April 2017).

O'Connor, J. 1968. Agrarian reforms in Cuba, 1959–1963. *Science & Society* 32(2), 169–217.

Patten, C. 1998. *East and West: The Last Governor of Hong Kong on Power, Freedom and the Future.* Basingstoke: Macmillan.

Pérez-López, J. 1986. Real economic growth in Cuba, 1965–1982. *The Journal of Developing Areas* 20(2), 151–172.

Pérez-López, J. 1991. *The Economics of Cuban Sugar*. University of Pittsburgh Press.

Pollitt, B. 1984. The Cuban sugar economy and the Great Depression, *Bulletin of Latin American Research* 3(2), 3–28.

Pollitt, B. 2004. The rise and fall of the Cuban sugar economy. *Journal of Latin American Studies* 36(2), 319–348.

Rabushka, A. 1973. *The Changing Face of Hong Kong: New Departures In Public Policy*. AEI-Hoover Policy Studies. Washington: American Enterprise Institute for Public Policy Research.

Rabushka, A. 1976. Value for money: the Hong Kong budgetary process. Hoover Institution Publication 152. Stanford, CA: Hoover Institution Press.

Rabushka, A. 1979. Hong Kong: a study in economic freedom. William H. Abbott Lectures in International Business and Economics. University of Chicago, Graduate School of Business.

Reid-Henry, S. 2009. *Fidel & Che: A Revolutionary Friendship*. London: Sceptre.

Ricardo, D. 1817. *On the Principles of Political Economy and Taxation*. London: John Murray.

Riedel, J. 1974. *The Industrialization of Hong Kong*. Tübingen: J. C. B. Mohr.

Roberts, R. 2014. *How Adam Smith Can Change Your Life*. London: Penguin.

Samuelson, P. 1961. *Economics: An Introductory Analysis,* 5th edition. New York: McGraw-Hill.

Samuelson, P. 1989. *Economics: An Introductory Analysis,* 13th edition. New York: McGraw-Hill.

BIBLIOGRAPHY

Schenk, C. 2001. *Hong Kong as an International Financial Centre: Emergence and Development 1945–1965*. London: Routledge.

Seaman, L. 1967. *Post-Victorian Britain 1902–1951*. London: Methuen.

Sinclair, M. 1968. *Viva Che!: Contributions in tribute to Ernesto 'Che' Guevara*. London: Lorrimer Publishing.

Smart, A. 2006. *The Shek Kip Mei Myth: Squatters, Fires and Colonial Rule in Hong Kong, 1950–1963*. Hong Kong University Press.

Smith, A. 1776. *An Inquiry into the Nature and Causes of the Wealth of Nations*. London: W. Strahan and T. Cadell.

Smith, H. 1966. *John Stuart Mill's Other Island: A Study of the Economic Development of Hong Kong*. London: Institute of Economic Affairs.

Snow, J. 1855. *On the Mode of Communication of Cholera,* 2nd edition. London: John Churchill.

Spencer, H. 1896. *The Study of Sociology*. New York: D. Appleton & Co.

Szczepanik, E. 1958. *The Economic Growth of Hong Kong*. Oxford University Press.

Szulc, T. 1986. *Fidel: A Critical Portrait*. New York: William Morrow.

Tablada Perez, C. 1990. *Che Guevara: Economics and Politics in the Transition to Socialism*. New York: Pathfinder.

Thomas, H. 19981. *Cuba, or the Pursuit of Freedom*. Boston, MA: Da Capo Press.

Thompson, E. 1963. *The Making of the English Working Class*. London: Victor Gollancz.

Thompson, E. 1966. History from below, *Times Literary Supplement*, 7 April.

Thorpe, A. 2001. *A History of the British Labour Party*. London: Palgrave.

Timmins, N. 2006. *The Five Giants: A Biography of the Welfare State*. New York: Harper Collins.

Tombs, R. 2014. *The English and Their History*. London: Penguin.

Tsang, S. 1988. *Democracy Shelved: Great Britain, China, and Attempts at Constitutional Reform in Hong Kong, 1945–1952*. Oxford University Press.

Tsang, S. 1995. *Government and Politics*. Hong Kong University Press.

Tsang, S. 2004. *A Modern History of Hong Kong*. London: I. B. Tauris.

Tsang, S. 2007. *Governing Hong Kong: Administrative Officers from the Nineteenth Century to the Handover to China, 1862–1997*. London: I. B. Tauris.

Tu, E. 2003. *Colonial Hong Kong in the Eyes of Elsie Tu*. Hong Kong University Press.

Ure, G. 2012. *Governors, Politics, and the Colonial Office: Public Policy in Hong Kong, 1918–58*. Hong Kong University Press.

Von Mises, L. 1935. Economic calculation in the socialist commonwealth. In *Collectivist Economic Planning*, F.A. Hayek (ed.), pp. 87–130. London: George Routledge & Sons.

Ward, M., and Devereux, J. 2010. The road not taken: pre-revolutionary Cuban living standards in comparative perspective. *The Journal of Economic History* 72(1), 104–132.

Welsh, F. 1997. *A History of Hong Kong*. London: HarperCollins.

Werlau, M. 2011. *Che Guevara Forgotten Victims*. Washington, DC: The Free Society Project.

Williamson, J. 1990. *What Washington means by policy reform?* Washington Institute for International Economics, Washington, DC.

Williamson, J. 2002. *Did the Washington Consensus Fail?* Outline of speech at the Centre for Strategic & International Studies, Washington, DC.

BIBLIOGRAPHY

Wood, J. 1996. *Alfred Marshall: Critical Assessments.* London: Taylor & Francis.

Yaffe, H. 2009. *Che Guevara: The Economics of Revolution.* London: Palgrave MacMillan.

Yueh, L. 2013. *China's Growth: The Making of an Economic Superpower.* Oxford University Press.

Zinn, H. 1980. *A People's History of the United States.* New York: Harper & Row.

ARCHIVAL SOURCES

UK National Archives, Public Records Office, Kew, London (PRO)
Hong Kong Government Record Service, Public Record Office, Hong Kong (HKRS)
Hong Kong Legislative Council Commission, Hansard (Hansard)
Hong Kong Census and Statistical Department (Censtatd)
Cuba Officina Nacional de Estadística e Información (ONEI)

IMAGE SOURCES

Figure 1, Figure 5, Figure 13, Figure 16 and Figure 17 are from Getty Images and are used with permission.

Figure 2, Figure 3, Figure 4, Figure 6, Figure 7, Figure 8 and Figure 12 are taken from public domain sources such as Wikimedia Commons.

ACKNOWLEDGEMENTS

I am grateful to Laurence, Hugo, Julie and Victoria and Chris for discussing Hong Kong and Cuba and their interest, thoughts and comments. They have been supportive throughout. And I would like to note my thanks to my parents and Katherine, Alex, Andrew and Carol. Many friends have been encouraging and contributed to this story and I would like to express my thanks to Stefano Quadrio-Curzio, Nick Viner, Andrew Gilchrist, Ben Smith, Mark and Ann-Marie Loveland, David Wood, Christoph Sander, Henry Elkington, Liz and John Buckingham, Drummond Hall, Peter Williamson, Warren Allderige, Nancy Amer, Rosanne Murisson and Joanne Horsfall.

I would like to thank Richard Baggaley at London Publishing Partnership for his very valuable comments and suggestions about the book and its structure, and Sam Clark and Emma Dain at T&T Productions for their editing and formatting and making the book much better than it would otherwise have been. I am particularly grateful to Roger Bootle for his thoughts and his insightful suggestions, to Stephen Bungay for discussions about philosophy and methodology and to Romesh Vaitilingam for his kind support.

We are all shaped by our interactions with friends, teachers and colleagues. My education was greatly enhanced by a number of teachers who were formative influences: John Kendall-Carpen-

ACKNOWLEDGEMENTS

ter; Walter Eltis, who sadly passed away this year; Galen Strawson, Andre Perold and Abraham Zaleznik; and many others. And at work I learnt much from Anthony Habgood, Barry Jones, Chris Hogg, Art Peck, Mark Joiner, Kate Swann, Steve Clarke and many, many others over the years. My colleagues at ASMC have always been supportive, and I thank Jo Whitehead, Mike Goold, Rebecca Homkes, Andrew Campbell and Marcus Alexander for their collegiality and their challenge.

INDEX

REVIEWS OF SAFE AS HOUSES?

Many people think that owning a house is a certain moneymaker, but this is not the historical experience. In his recent book *Safe as Houses? A Historical Analysis of Property Prices*, Neil Monnery presents data from an array of nations going back (in some cases) several centuries. What he discovers is that real house prices have generally been flat over time, or have increased by at most 1% a year. Rather like gold, then, house prices have been a good store of value rather than an automatic route to riches.
The Economist

Anybody interested in the housing market and in trying to preserve their wealth in these uncertain times should take a look at a fascinating new book: *Safe as Houses: A Historical Analysis of Property Prices* is full of useful facts.
Allister Heath, City A.M.

A must read if you are remotely interested in the history of house prices.
Merryn Somerset Webb, Money Week

Neil Monnery's *Safe as Houses?* is one of the few sane books on housing economics.
Sir Simon Jenkins, The Spectator

REVIEWS OF ARCHITECT OF PROSPERITY

During the 1960s, governments were responding to political un-
rest and economic challenges with nationalisation, centralised
planning and public spending (financed by heavy taxes and
debt). There was intense pressure for Sir John Cowperthwaite,
the financial secretary of Hong Kong, to join the crowd.... A
new biography of Cowperthwaite by Neil Monnery, a former
management consultant, tells of a man who replied to these de-
mands with a qualified 'no', and in the process became that most
unusual of things: a bureaucrat hero to libertarians. His approach
would subsequently be labelled 'positive non-interventionism',
meaning governance stopping just short of laissez-faire.
The Economist

Not before time we now have a fascinating book on one of those
who helped create Hong Kong's thriving economy. Cowperthwaite was a believer in free market economics well before this
idea became popular again. Hong Kong should be grateful to
him.
Lord Patten of Barnes, last governor of Hong Kong

There are figures in history who deserve to be far better known
and Sir John Cowperthwaite is one of those. Neil Monnery's account of the way he shaped Hong Kong into a dynamic and successful economy now far more prosperous than its colonial
ruler, Britain, is all the more fascinating in the light of the current

debate about what drives economic development. Policymakers today can learn a lot from the focus and the willingness to ignore the conventional wisdom of the time demonstrated by Cowperthwaite and his colleagues.

Diane Coyle, professor of economics at the University of Manchester

Hong Kong went from being a barren rock with no resources to becoming a dynamic economy with living standards higher than many European countries. A key role in this remarkable story was played by Sir John Cowperthwaite as Financial Secretary. He believed that expenditure should be determined by revenues, not the other way round, that private enterprise should decide where investment should be allocated, tax rates should be low to attract capital and create surplus profits to be re-invested to create compounding growth. He was against deficits because he viewed the taxpayer of tomorrow just as worthy as the taxpayer of today. The results were spectacular and made Hong Kong into the economic miracle it is today. This book charts his wonderful, inspiring and remarkable story and his philosophy is brilliantly expressed. The wonder is that other Governments in Europe don't follow this example.

Lord Lamont of Lerwick, former Chancellor of the Exchequer

I have just read a fascinating new book called *Architect of Prosperity* by Neil Monnery. It's about the role of Sir John Cowperthwaite, Financial Secretary of Hong Kong from 1961 to 1971 in setting the colony on the road to prosperity. It is an astonishing story… Its success derived from brilliant economic policymaking that involved reliance on market forces and minimising the role of the state… You might think that, given the economic record, Britain's economic establishment, including the serried ranks of mandarins and their political masters, might feel that they have a good deal to learn. They have. They should read Monnery's book.

Roger Bootle, The Daily Telegraph

Sir John Cowperthwaite, who arrived in Hong Kong in 1945 and topped off his career there as financial secretary from 1961 to 1971, was not one to blow his own trumpet and never cultivated a coterie of followers to do it for him. Thankfully, however, Neil Monnery has now published the first biography of Cowperthwaite. Cowperthwaite, a Scotsman by birth, was at the heart of economic policymaking in Hong Kong throughout this period and the colony's success was largely attributable to his particular brand of free-market economics. For those interested in economic management, it is a remarkable tale, and one that Monnery tells with relish.

Richard Cockett, The Literary Review

There's a book just out which everyone in the Conservative party ought to read: *Architect of Prosperity* by Neil Monnery. It's the biography of one of the 20th century's greatest unsung heroes, Sir John Cowperthwaite, the financial secretary in the British colonial administration whose determinedly low-tax, regulation-light, fiscally austere regime put Hong Kong on its path to prosperity.

James Delingpole, The Spectator

Anyone seeking to understand the true nature of inequality must read Neil Monnery's excellent book. In Hong Kong Sir John Cowperthwaite created a society of great wealth inequality but of great freedom and opportunity. Refugees fled to Hong Kong from the imposed equality of the People's Republic of China in pursuit of the greater equality of opportunity in the British Colony. This book raises fundamental questions about the nature of the equality we seek to pursue.

Russell Napier, market historian

This book tells the story of Hong Kong's success, focusing on the career of Sir John Cowperthwaite who played key roles in the colony's administration from 1945 to 1971. ...Monnery tells the story with verve and accuracy, providing one of the best compact economic histories of Hong Kong in the second half of the twentieth century.

Professor Jack A. Goldstone, Economic Affairs

This fascinating account of the rise of Hong Kong as a global economic powerhouse is well written and, as such, easy to read and understand. I'm happy to recommend it wholeheartedly to CapX's discerning readership...[Neil Monnery's] work has immortalised a man to whom so many owe so much. *Architect of Prosperity* is an economic and intellectual history. Above all, it is a tribute to a principled, self-effacing, consequential and deeply moral man. Monnery deserves our gratitude for writing it.

Marian L. Tupy, CapX

Architect of Prosperity won the Gold Medal for best Biography at the Axiom Book Awards (2018).